ACKNOWLEDGEMENTS

Special thanks to those who helped me with the process of writing this memoir: Matt Gill, Christina Cundiff, Michelle Monet, Laura Phillips, Susan Huber Sullivan, Noosha Ravaghi, all my beta readers and the Medium writing community.

While the stories in this book are true, some names and dates have been changed in the interest of privacy.

Written for my children.

TIN MAN: "What have you learned, Dorothy?"

DOROTHY: "Well, I think it wasn't enough just to want to see Uncle Henry and Auntie Em, and it's that — if I ever go looking for my heart's desire, I won't look any further than my own backyard. Because if it isn't there, I never really lost it to begin with. Is that right?"

GLINDA: "That's all it is."

The Wizard of Oz, 1939, script by Noel Langley, Florence Ryerson and Edgar Allen Woolf. Based on the book by L. Frank Baum.

Chapter One

Five words and my whole world exploded.

"Glenna, I'm just not happy."

Eric's sentence repeated itself in my head as I crossed the living room and sat on the black leather couch next to him. I prayed he wouldn't say the two extra words that hung in the air between us, *"with you."*

My throat tightened all of a sudden, leaving me barely able to swallow. A surge of adrenaline rushed through my body in a fight-or-flight response. The first stirrings of a panic attack disabled me from saying anything in response.

It was Saturday night. Our two little boys, Brandon and Shawn, were staying over at Eric's mother's house to give us a date night. I'd waited most of the afternoon for Eric to suggest a place for dinner. He always did when we had an evening alone, but this time the last traces of daylight faded without a word from him. There was a strange vibe in the house after the boys left with Grandma. Eric sat in silence in front of the TV watching Entertainment Tonight, a show he hated and usually called "mindless trash."

When he finally spoke again, Eric treated me to a compilation of things he wasn't happy about. All of them had to do with me, things I'd done wrong over the fifteen years of our marriage. I listened and tried to keep my hands steady so he wouldn't notice them shaking.

Eric never talked like this before, not even close. In fact, he was more likely to shut down rather than share his feelings. I'd learned to accept the silent treatment over the years and wait it out until he wasn't upset anymore.

In all our time together, Eric and I never had a single knockdown, drag-out fight. Neither of us wanted to rock the boat. We were high school sweethearts. I thought we would be best friends forever. Now he made it sound like I was his worst enemy.

Eric said I was selfish. We didn't have sex enough. My cooking was terrible. I spent too much money on the Visa card. My mood swings were out of control. I wasn't responsive to his needs. We never had fun anymore. The list seemed to go on forever. Shouldn't I have known these things already? It would be the first of many times I was left unsure of myself.

There was only one question after that. Like me, Eric had not been single since we were both in our teens. Surely he wouldn't be talking this way unless he already had someone else in my place. Memories flashed from the last couple of months that hadn't added up, like waking up in the middle of the night and finding Eric in the living room talking in hushed tones on the house phone. There was also that time he called me on a Friday night at the last minute to say he was going out with "the guys." What about when he took the garbage out with his cell phone in his hand? The brutal truth smacked me hard across the face, and there was nothing left to do but ask.

"Is there somebody else?" I tried to sound

non-confrontational, knowing Eric wouldn't tolerate accusations.

He paused and sighed loudly. "Yes, but…"

Eric looked away from me as he explained his cheating wasn't the reason we were having this conversation. "It's not about her," he said. My stomach retched, and I crossed my arms over it to keep from vomiting. The idea of a "her" was sickening. Eric warned me not to blame his new girlfriend because none of this was her fault. He claimed he was already miserable because of the way I treated him. "I couldn't take it anymore," he whined. He sounded like a martyr, the poor suffering husband forced to put up with his cruel wife.

"I'm going to stay with my parents for now," he added, still without looking at me.

I moved myself away from him then, instead choosing to sit down on the hardwood floor beneath me. Eric had installed the wood panels the year before when we had moved into the new house. It was our dream home, built from the ground up just for our family. We lived in the city of Jupiter Farms, a place where there were actual farms. We were as likely to see a horse trotting down the street as a car driving by. Our house was beautiful, spacious and modern with a saltwater pool in the backyard. Every day living there with Eric and our two young boys was a blessing.

As Eric continued his speech, every word was like a knife in my heart. I needed him to stop talking so I could curl up into a ball and vanish. He made me feel like the meanest person on earth.

His new girlfriend was someone he worked with, the receptionist in the land surveying office he managed. I almost laughed through my tears as he confessed. It was such an obvious cliche, something Eric and I would normally roll our eyes about if it happened to somebody else. Eric described his new girl as younger than me with pink hair, which he proudly offered as evidence of his newfound coolness. I didn't even ask her name. Eric was a walking midlife crisis. That's what I wanted to shout at the top of my lungs, but instead I sat and cried with my head in my hands while he watched me.

Eric and I were the couple everybody envied. People said we would beat the odds and make it to at least our silver anniversary. His mother and stepfather were the only real family I had ever since I was a teenager. The word divorce was never spoken once before in our household. None of this was supposed to happen.

Lost in my grief, Eric's voice startled me. "Do you want anything from McDonald's?"

I looked up into his bright green eyes as if he had spoken in French. Didn't he see how upset I was? I was falling into a black hole of despair. He was hungry for fast food as cheap as his affair.

"No thanks." I managed to answer.

Eric snatched his keys off the kitchen table with a loud scraping noise and vanished through the back door.

After he was gone, I paced aimlessly

around the house. My anxiety was full force and getting worse, making it hard to take a normal breath. Everything in our home looked spotless as it always did. I took time to clean it with loving care. We had great memories in the house as a family even though we hadn't been living there long. There were pool parties and goofing off with the boys and lounging around watching movies together. Yet I suddenly felt the urge to run as far and fast as I could. Without Eric, the house might as well be haunted with ghosts.

I was 35 years old and had never lived by myself in my entire life. I'd moved as a teenager straight from my mom's house to living with Eric and then marrying him. For the first time in my life, I had to contemplate being a single mother with two small children. I'd never even done my own taxes or changed a spare tire by myself. Eric always took care of everything, and I never bothered to learn since he was always supposed to be there.

Eric didn't care how much I still loved him. I was about to lose him and the only

real family I had ever known. Everything I
knew and believed in was gone within a
ten-minute conversation.   What the hell was
I going to do?

Chapter Two

Eric and I became friends in the eleventh grade at Pompano Beach High School. That was the year I dropped out of school at my mother's insistence. I'd been frequently skipping classes, and my mom told me I was wasting my time and needed to get a job and pay rent instead. The day I dropped out, I ran into Eric as I was going from class to class returning my textbooks. He walked with me all over the school, telling me it made him sad that I had to quit and miss out on everything.

We began dating that summer. Eric picked me up every morning and drove me to the mall where I was working at Sears in the Key Shop. He was kind, funny and most of all responsible, a quality that was sorely lacking from my life. When I had a curfew, he made sure I always got home on time even though I begged to stay out longer.

Eric was stable and sound where I was reckless. When we were both seventeen, he asked me to stop drinking alcohol because he felt my partying was out of control. It never occurred to me to question whether he was right, so I listened to him and quit altogether. With minimal supervision at home from my mother, I leaned on Eric more and more. He gave my life structure where there once was none.

When I turned seventeen, my mom started dating a man with schizophrenia named Glenn who later moved into our small apartment. He was creepy, borderline insane and suggestive toward me to the point where I didn't want to be home at all. I often spent the night at Eric's parents' house. Eric would smuggle me in and then sneak me out the next morning.

When my mother finally kicked me out of our apartment for staying out every night, I lied about my age and moved into a studio apartment close to the beach with Eric. We lived on peanut butter and jelly sandwiches bought with our sparse paychecks and watched an old black and white TV for entertainment. I studied and got my GED on my own when I was eighteen. Eric skipped college and went straight into land surveying. We got married on a hot summer day in 1989, after living together for three years. I thought being Eric's wife was the thing I wanted most in the world.

My relationship with my mother was always tumultuous. She had a lifelong history of mental illness and alcoholism. I learned not to depend on her for things at a young age. By the time I got to high school, it was like having a roommate instead of a parent in the house. She seemed to like Eric and said she was happy about our marriage, but I wondered if she was just glad to have me off her hands.

We didn't speak much over the years that followed because when we did, I always ended up feeling bad about myself. It seemed almost unnatural to discuss my personal life with her. I knew she'd either laugh at whatever I said or gossip about it to distant family members. There were times I carried a lot of guilt about not reaching out to her more often in adulthood. It simply seemed better to remain acquaintances.

By contrast, I adored my father. He was the only person who ever loved me unconditionally. I was by his side at the hospital when he passed away from heart failure. Shawn was only six months old when my dad died. It broke my heart my little boy wouldn't remember his grandfather. Brandon was four, and I hoped he might remember little flashes of my dad. They would never play Black Jack for hours while munching on stick pretzels and cracking jokes the way I did growing up with him. The boys would miss out on his long heartfelt talks and the feeling they could tell him anything. My father's death broke my heart even though I knew it was coming because his health was bad. I missed him every single day with the tremendous loss only a little girl can feel.

Eric was at the center of everything. I felt grateful for his guidance as I became a young adult trying to navigate the world, having learned very little in my mother's home. Eric's parents and siblings were the family I never had, taking me in and loving me as if I were one of their own. When Eric taught me how to drive, his mother Elaine took me to get my license and out to lunch to celebrate. She was also there when I picked out my wedding dress at David's Bridals. I felt so fortunate to have her as my mother-in-law. She nurtured me the way my own mother could not.

Eric and I waited for almost a decade to have kids, focusing mostly on our careers. I took classes at a technical school to become a medical transcriptionist so I could stay at home with our future children. After I graduated, I opened my own transcription company and quickly filled it with doctor clients. Eric was promoted to being his company's office manager. People saw us not just as husband and wife but also the best of friends. Eric and I made each other laugh like nobody else. When we decided to add a child to our family, we both felt excited but nervous about how being parents would change our lives. Neither one of us had much experience with children, but we had plenty of love to give.

The day I finally took a positive pregnancy test fell on the same day as Eric's birthday. I found an unused box in our garage and bought a pair of light blue baby booties to put inside it. Then I wrapped the whole box with colorful paper and a giant bow on top. When Eric opened his gift, he was happy but overwhelmed. I shared his concerns about raising a child. For the next nine months, I read every baby book on the market and thought I was as prepared as I could be. I dreamed of all the things I'd teach my son or daughter about the world. My plan was to be a safe place to land as a mother who would always understand them no matter what.

Brandon was born in the winter of 1998, a beautiful blue-eyed baby who barely fussed at all. I felt almost manic with happiness in the hospital, but after I was discharged I had postpartum depression that struck me with the force of a swinging fist, knocking me flat and leaving me unable to care for myself or my newborn son. Eric took care of everything with the help of his family. I cried constantly and blamed myself for getting sick. What kind of mother can't take care of her baby? I'd hide in the bedroom shaking with anxiety and away from my own child. Every time I heard Eric's family downstairs playing with Brandon and cooing at him, it tore me up inside. Whenever they brought the baby to see me, he was always freshly bathed and in brand new outfits. It killed me that I wasn't the one doing those things for him. I couldn't even change his diaper by myself.

When I saw my obstetrician for my postpartum checkup and explained the situation, he prescribed an antidepressant and suggested I go to a psychologist. I would have done anything to stop the depression before it swallowed me whole. The combination of medication and behavioral therapy worked, and soon I was taking care of Brandon full time and loving every minute. Eric said he was relieved that I was my old self again. Both of us were ready to move on from the episode and enjoy our new family.

Shawn was born four years after Brandon. When I got pregnant for the second time, Eric and I both worried that I'd have another depressive episode. My doctor told me the antidepressant I took was safe for pregnancy, so I got through Shawn's birth relatively unscathed. It was important to us that Brandon have a little brother so he wouldn't be alone in the world. Brandon was only four, but he constantly doted on Shawn and wanted to spend every waking moment with him. In turn, Shawn worshiped Brandon and wanted to do everything his big brother did. Their relationship was everything I dreamed it would be.

About six months after Shawn was born, I had another depressive episode that was so severe I nearly attempted suicide. My therapist told me I'd likely suffer from episodes of depression and anxiety for the rest of my life. She said I had a chemical imbalance in my brain and that medication was crucial to keeping the illness at bay.

She also referred me to a psychiatrist who diagnosed me with bipolar II disorder, which is similar to bipolar disorder but involves fewer manic episodes and more depression. The psychiatrist told me I could expect the symptoms I was having to continue to some degree for the rest of my life. If I ever stopped my medication, the doctor warned, I'd likely try to kill myself.

Eric was my biggest support during all of it. He read everything he could get his hands on about mental illness so he could understand it better. His parents were both psychologists, so he talked to them about the best way to help me manage my depression and anxiety. When symptoms broke through my medication, I wept and shivered while Eric comforted me. He told me I was strong and would get through it, but instead I felt weak inside.

Mental illness was chipping away at my life one episode at a time and taking its toll on me. I was constantly on guard about having another breakdown, maybe one that couldn't be stopped this time. As a mom of two young boys, I did my best to take care of my mental health, but their needs often came before mine and were sometimes overwhelming. Even when I didn't have full-blown depression, there were days lost to crippling anxiety and a sadness I couldn't shake.

Brandon, Shawn and Eric were my entire life. I took good care of them, keeping the house clean and feeding them and taking the boys to their soccer games. On my good days, I devoted every second to making sure they were happy. If Eric was ever unhappy, he never mentioned it to me. I thought our family would live the rest of our lives in the protective loving bubble I had created around us that nothing could touch. Except the bubble wasn't real. It was just a vision I had created in my chemically imbalanced mind, fragile and ready to burst at any time.

Chapter Three

After Eric's confession, we spent the night in separate rooms. I sat cross-legged on our king-sized bed in the dark, half awake between fuzzy dreams. It would be the first of many nights I'd battle insomnia.

When Eric showed up in our bedroom at first light, he avoided my eyes as he packed his suitcase.

"I'm going to go stay with my parents," he reminded me. "I'll bring the boys home this afternoon. We can just tell them that Daddy is moving out for a while."

I felt a fresh set of tears well up. Brandon was a six-year-old first grader and Shawn only two. How could I explain something to my sweet little boys I couldn't understand myself?

I watched Eric's gray SUV pull out of the driveway and disappear down the street. Then I hurried to the bedroom closet to inspect the clothes he left behind. If he didn't take a lot with him, maybe he only wanted to be gone a few days. I spotted a few dress shirts and a pair of faded jeans. Reaching forward, I embraced them all together on their hangers. They were soft and smelled like my husband. *This is crazy*, I thought as I hugged them tighter. Since the age of sixteen, Eric had been part of my life almost every day. He was my other half, my biggest supporter, my hero. Life without him was unthinkable.

The next thing I did was call my best friend, Susan, who lived in North Carolina. She gasped in between sobs when I told her about Eric's affair. Susan, Eric and I were best friends as teenagers in Pompano Beach. We used to hang out at the 16th Street beach at night, get wasted on Coors, then sneak onto the property of the nearest hotel. We'd sit out by the pool talking to guests from all over the world until our curfews passed. It was hard to believe twenty years had gone by. It was the same length of time since I'd had Coors or any other alcoholic drink.

I was still talking to Susan when I heard the back door swing open with a bang against the kitchen wall, followed by a little voice crying. Hanging up the phone, I leapt off the bed and nearly ran into Brandon. His cheeks were crimson and dotted with tears. I scooped him up instinctively.

"Oh honey, everything will be okay. Please don't worry, little lamb. Your daddy and I love you so much."

I shot a wide-eyed look at Eric, who blushed and lowered his head. He held Shawn in his arms. I could see the confusion on my younger son's baby face, trying to figure out why his brother was hysterical.

"What did you do?" I demanded of Eric, already knowing the answer.

"I told them on the way home."

"You told our sons you were moving out of the house while you were driving?" I felt my face flush with unfamiliar anger.

"No," he admitted. "I pulled over to the side of the road and told them."

"Why would you be so cold to them?" I felt confused and disgusted. *What must the boys be thinking?*

Eric sighed. "Because I didn't want them to see you falling apart."

Brandon complained then that his stomach hurt, so I carried him into his bedroom so he could lie down. I rubbed his stomach with one hand and his sandy blond hair with the other while I whispered softly in his ear to reassure him. *This is what's truly important,* I thought as I closed my tired eyes.
My children matter most of all.

Brandon surrendered after a while and fell asleep. I shut his door and found Eric still pacing in the living room. He didn't look my way, but he let out a large dramatic sigh.

"I wonder what's wrong with Brandon's stomach," he asked. *Was he serious?*

"What did you say to them?" I blurted out as a response.

"I just said, you know, sometimes people get divorced."

There it was, the D word. Neither one of us had said it out loud yet. I still hoped *My Eric* would return, the Eric who would never have a seedy affair or destroy the person who adored him more than anything. Because *this* Eric I could not deal with. We were utter strangers.

Once I persuaded him that Brandon would be okay, Eric headed back to his parents' house. I didn't watch him drive away this time, too anxious to go to the window. It was official. I was a single mom living with two young children, and I was scared to death.

Later in the day, a knock at my front door interrupted the game I was playing with Shawn. I opened it to find Eric's mother and stepfather standing before me in tears. His mother, Elaine, reached out and took me in her arms.

"I want you to know," she sobbed, "that you will *always* be our daughter."

We all stayed quiet for a minute after that, but the three of us felt the water and not blood that flowed between us. We needed to believe nothing had changed.

That night, with both boys in bed, I tried again to sleep with no luck. It was getting late, and the next day was Monday. Massive anxiety was making it hard to sit still. I grabbed the phone and hit redial.

"Susan, I don't know what to do," I cried. "Tomorrow is Monday."

"Right?" Susan said as she tried to understand.

"I have to get the boys ready for school."

"Okay?"

"I...I've never done that by myself before. Eric has always helped me."

Poor Susan had her work cut out for her trying to comfort me. I felt as helpless as little Shawn.

"Glenna," she said, "I've known you forever. I know this scares you, but I also know you can DO this! You WILL get those kids to school! It may not look perfect or pretty, but I know you will get them there."

I thanked Susan and hung up, trying to plan everything out. By the time Monday morning came, I was drunk with exhaustion, but I got off the couch and did what Susan told me. She was right. It wasn't pretty at all. I tried to block out my intense grief as I hurried to get the boys ready and prayed they didn't notice me crying from the backseat of the car. We got to the school five minutes late, but I still counted it as a drop in the bottom of the empty bucket that held my self-confidence.

More than anything, I wanted Eric to come back home. Maybe if I held everything together, he would return to a woman who wasn't so needy and weak. I could promise to work on myself and change for the better. Maybe he'd even love me again. I held the thought like a life raft on the ocean of lies I let myself believe.

Chapter Four

Walking into the spacious townhouse for the first time since signing the escrow papers, I felt a rush of new excitement. The place was beautiful with light-colored walls and carpet that played off the dark-blue granite counter tops. I happily sorted through mental images of my furniture in each room. It was fun to imagine the boys playing games together and barreling up and down the upstairs hallway. The townhouse was the first place I ever owned all by myself. It was brand new, like my life.

Four months had passed since Eric's confession. He was now living with the pink-haired receptionist. Her name was Michelle, not that it mattered. He tried to come back twice to reunite with me, both times teary and apologetic and swearing that his affair was over. I gratefully took him back both times even though I knew he merely felt guilty and had no intention of working on our marriage. His moral code brought him back home, not his love for me. He was determined to do the right thing, no matter how wrong the right thing was for both of us.

During our final reconciliation, we took the boys on a camping weekend with Brandon's Boy Scout troop. Eric and I sat around the campfire together with the other parents after the kids went to bed. I felt a burning in the pit of my stomach knowing that Eric didn't want to be there with me. The whole trip revolved around my paralyzing anxiety and his betrayal.

Eric and I had plenty of room on the campground to avoid each other. We used little Shawn's boundless energy to keep us distracted by chasing him around on the grass. The whole weekend reeked of false appearances and rejection and trying to create happiness where there was none. I knew deep down that Eric wished the receptionist were sitting by the fire sharing marshmallows with him instead.

Later, back in the cabin, I accused Eric of not loving me. He rolled his eyes and said I was being too sensitive. My gut instinct told me otherwise.

Early the next morning, I packed up little Shawn and left to go home. I felt bad about spoiling Brandon's trip, but if I'd had to pretend everything was perfect any longer, I would have had a nervous breakdown. Leaving camp that morning was the first of many times I would disappoint my oldest son.

Shawn and I waited near the front window of our house all day until Eric brought Brandon home. When Brandon went directly to his room, my younger son sensed tension and followed him asking to play.

"What exactly do you want me to do"? Eric made a show of throwing his hands up, looking flustered.

I wanted him to feel passionate about me. I wanted him to ache without me. It wasn't what I asked him for, though. That would be like asking a fish to walk on land. There was no recognition in Eric's face for the things I wanted. The Eric I once knew no longer existed. After eighteen years together, he was a total stranger.

"I want you to leave, take time to think and figure out what you want." I tried to sound brave even though my voice was trembling.

Eric wasted no time once I'd given him permission. He gathered his things and exited our house within the hour. He moved into the receptionist's apartment the same night and never left.

After Eric was gone for good, I spent my time trying. I tried to get the kids to school on time without them seeing me cry. I tried to focus on my transcription job until I couldn't drag myself to the computer anymore. I tried to trick myself into eating by rushing down food and praying it wouldn't come back up. I tried not to fall apart when the check engine light came on in my car and I didn't know what it meant. I tried not to care when Eric emailed me and said we should ignore our upcoming sixteenth wedding anniversary "for everyone's sake."

Most of all, I tried not to let clinical depression take over. My boys needed me to be stable, but my mental illness was unsympathetic. It made me wonder how much my bipolar disorder had to do with Eric's decision to break up with me. Whenever the symptoms struck, they were unrelenting and cruel, causing me to weep and shudder and hide in bed.

I'd always done my best to hide how I was feeling from Eric and the boys so I wouldn't scare them; however, some days it was all too obvious. There were times I couldn't focus or keep the house as spotless as I liked it. Other times, I could cry in the bathroom and get away with it, wiping my tears and returning to my family before they noticed I was gone.

Eric continued to come by the house every Sunday afternoon to relax on the couch and watch NASCAR. The rest of the week was devoted to his midlife crisis, but on Sundays he'd stretch out at "home" with a beer. While he sat there, he told me stories of clubs and bars he'd been to the night before. He complained about being exhausted from staying out all night.

"Have you ever eaten at Denny's at three o'clock in the morning?" he bragged. "It's so much fun."

I hated Eric for using me and the kids to recharge his batteries. "You need to choose," I said in an angry voice one Sunday as I sat down next to him. Eric turned away from the race cars and seemed surprised to see me there looking dead serious. I gave him a week to answer, either give up Michelle or we divorce. It was the ultimate bluff, but I hoped he wouldn't catch on.

I didn't hear much from Eric until he showed up a week later as requested. We went out back to sit on the deck by our saltwater pool that nobody swam in anymore. The water was swampy and green from lack of care. It still made me think of Brandon and Shawn swimming across it like little fishes, but I wasn't in the mood for such memories. I sat down across from Eric and waited with my arms folded across my body in self-protection.

He spoke at almost a whisper. "I'm not ready to give up my relationship with

Michelle."

I jumped to my feet and slid my patio chair back so hard it fell over with a resounding bang. "Divorce it IS!" I shouted behind me as I walked inside toward the bedroom where Eric could no longer see me. A few seconds later, I heard the back door slam. My chest tightened and tears formed in my eyes as I realized he'd called my bluff. That conversation was the last time Eric and I would ever talk about "us."

Word got around Jupiter Farms about our breakup. I received overzealous sympathy hugs while grocery shopping. The other soccer moms hovered over me with stark fear in their eyes for their own marriages. I was proof it could happen to anyone.

"I'd kill my husband if he ever did that," they said smartly, smug in the fantasy that *their* husbands would never stoop so low. The affair might be contagious, though, and as a newly separated woman I might be a threat around their men.

The ladies' support quickly waned, but it didn't bother me that much. I'd never been into small talk, which was the extent of my relationships with these women. I was never very good at being a soccer mom, anyway. Most of the other moms annoyed me with their endless prattle about recipes and housecleaning. They also gossiped about each other when one of them wasn't around. I was the subject of that gossip now, and I felt both ashamed and dangerous.

I briefly considered moving back to Pompano Beach, where I still had friends and lots of good memories. When I announced my plans to Eric's horrified parents, Elaine and Don, they frantically listed the reasons I should stay in Jupiter Farms. I knew they were worried about their relationship with their grandsons. They just couldn't see the ghosts that haunted my house.

"My support system is in Pompano," I tried to explain to my in-laws.

"WE are your support system!" Don shot back, his fist smacking my dining room table. I decided not to point out that Michelle was now sitting in my seat at their Sunday dinners.

Still, I believed Eric's stepfather enough not to follow through with my plan. I would still sell the house and move out, but just to the other side of Jupiter. I'd move into one of the elegant new townhouses in the Abacoa community. My real estate agent, Grace, drove me around to look at places. Grace sold Eric and me the land we'd built our dream house on just a few years earlier. She felt pity for me now, although she tried to make the search fun with her cheery optimism.

When I put the haunted house up for sale, I hoped it wouldn't be obvious that a marriage died there. It seemed like a bad omen. Nobody seemed to notice, though, and the house sold in record time. I worried it would be hard for the boys to move away from their friends, but I honestly believed a new start was exactly what we all needed. Every time I walked into our family room, I remembered sitting on the wood floor getting dumped by the man who was supposed to love me forever. I couldn't even sleep in the bed Eric and I once shared. He was everywhere in that house, but nowhere at the same time.

Waiting for the moving van to arrive, I looked forward to making all the decisions about where my furniture would go. This time, there would be no input from anyone else. The world seemed fresh and full of possibility, and I prayed it would be enough to replace the blackness that festered within my heart.

It was the first time since the separation that I felt a spark of hope. I wanted to savor it. Now was the time to change everything, not just where we lived but within me, too. It felt like I finally had some good news. I couldn't have known it was also bad news.

Chapter Five

I brought the apple martini to my lips,
tasting the sweet mixed with sour, trying not
to drink too fast. I'd already had two rum
and Cokes back at the townhouse to steel my
nerves, and I didn't want to be too tipsy to
drive home, if I ended up going home at all.
Brandon and Shawn were safe with Elaine
for the night. Feigning impatience, I sat on a
bench in front of a bar and grill tapping the
heel of my pointy black boot on the
sidewalk. Every so often, I'd let out a large
sigh.

My new neighborhood, Abacoa, had a
town center with little specialty shops and
restaurants dotting its Main Street. It was the
end of August, still warm and muggy
outside. The setting Florida sun was
throwing pinks and purples up into the sky
and casting shadows up and down the
walkway. I tried to seem aloof as people
walked past me. There were couples
laughing together and groups of men and
women still in their work clothes enjoying
the last moments of happy hour. If I caught

someone's eye, I offered a slight smile and nod. I wondered if they thought I looked cheap in my short black skirt and lace-up boots, not willing to admit to myself it was part of the plan.

Standing up again, I took my phone out of my purse to check the time. Rolling my eyes in pretend disgust, I let out another loud sigh and looked one way up the street and down the other. A light evening breeze swept across my skin. After a while, I noticed the restaurant staff sneaking sympathetic glances at me. One waiter, a guy barely in his 20s who looked as good as he probably thought he did, came outside for a cigarette and addressed my frustration.

"He didn't show up?"

There was a friendly tone to his words that I instantly hated. I imagined he used the same breezy voice to announce the daily specials to customers. It was hard to tell whether he was mocking me. His name tag said Doug. He looked like a Doug, all cocky and sure of himself.

Shrugging my shoulders at Doug, I walked away from the restaurant. I felt sheepish and embarrassed that he believed I'd been stood up. Once I reached the parking garage, I felt my eyes getting hotter and wetter. Doug was wrong. I hadn't been waiting for somebody at that restaurant. Instead, I was waiting for anybody. My desperate aching for human contact made me feel ashamed. I hated myself for being so stupid. All that had come of my plan was people like Doug who felt sorry for me. Pity was the last thing I wanted.

When I got back to the townhouse, I finished the last of the rum and Coke I'd stashed, hoping it would help me sleep at least for a while. Alcohol hadn't become an everyday occurrence yet, but I found it was excellent in a pinch as an emotional painkiller. I'd forgotten about that in the years I was sober at Eric's insistence. He never thought I could handle my alcohol. It had been so long since I'd had any, I couldn't remember if he was right.

My first drink off the wagon was at the same bar I'd just walked away from. It happened the same day my divorce from Eric was final. I remembered the friendly lady bartender setting the martini glass in front of me like it was nothing. My hand was unsteady as I picked up the glass with the apple-flavored liquid sloshing around the rim. I decided then it would become my signature drink. Taking my first sip, I raised my glass to eye level for a silent toast. *Happy divorce day!*

Eric didn't show up at the courthouse for our divorce hearing. I ended up going with my real estate agent, Grace, and sobbing throughout the entire thing. Grace offered to take me to lunch after it was all over. I felt grateful for her kindness, but I declined, made an awkward excuse, hugged her and left. My eyes were soaked with tears from crying. There was no way I could put into words how devastated I was in the courtroom. The need to be alone was overwhelming, alone with a martini. *Fuck you, Eric.*

Soon after the divorce was final, new credit cards arrived in my mailbox. Eric and I always had impeccable credit, mainly due to his diligence in paying bills on time. The card companies must have caught wind that we'd split up and mailed me offers in my own name. *Good for emergencies*, I decided, activating each one as they arrived. I soon discovered that shopping was a great stress reliever. I'd hit the mall on weekends, then go home and order clothes for myself and Christmas presents for the boys on the internet.

It helped to focus on something pretty and forget for a while, even when I sometimes felt shopper's remorse. I justified my actions by being determined that Christmas would be like any other for the boys except without both parents under the same roof. Brandon and Shawn were both so excited about the upcoming holiday, and I threw myself into making it the best one ever.

Jasper came to live with us in the fall, a fluffy brown Wheaten Terrier puppy who lit the boys' blue eyes up like sparklers. None of us could seem to stop petting him, and he seemed forever grateful as he basked in the love of his new family. Sure, he'd been expensive, but the $800 I spent on him was worth every penny to see my kids so happy. We started crate training him with the help of pet care books, showering him with positive attention when he did his business outside. He was the sweetest thing any of us had ever seen.

"What was your favorite thing today?"

I always asked this of Brandon and Shawn when I tucked them into bed at night in the room they shared. They were four years apart in age, and I knew they wouldn't always want to share a room. Still, I believed the best parts of life were the little ones, like giggling late at night in the dark with your brother. I wanted them to know no matter what the world threw at them, they would always have each other.

"Christmas is coming!" Shawn yelled as he threw off his covers and jumped up and down on his bed. I envied his never dwindling energy. The kid always kept me entertained. Jasper didn't appreciate the bouncing and hurried away for a quieter sleeping space.

Brandon sat up in his bed and agreed, "Christmas is going to rock!" I smiled back at him, thinking about the gifts I'd bought him and Shawn. I hoped they would love them.

Eric took the boys to his new condo every other weekend and every Wednesday for overnight stays. He pulled up for the first visitation with Michelle in the passenger's seat, and I nearly collapsed in the sting of watching her drive away with Eric and our children. I still felt like Eric owed me something, so I jealously sent him an email telling him never to bring Michelle to my townhouse again. It was petty, but I told him I couldn't stand to look at her. He respected my wishes and came alone from then on, despite complaining I was causing conflict in his new relationship.

My former in-laws stayed in close contact with me, but things between us were getting more strained when they came to visit. I'm sure they didn't appreciate the comments I let slip out about their golden son, once calling him a "living, breathing sexual harassment suit." However, the brunt of my anger was saved for the receptionist. Elaine once mentioned in passing that Michelle had been sick with a cold.

"Good," I shot back. "I hope she DIES!"

Feeling bitter was an emotion I wasn't comfortable with. Harsh words popped out of my mouth sometimes before I could stuff them back down. I'd always held my tongue with Eric, but now there was no boat left to overturn. He had already made that crystal clear.

"I don't want to be friends with you," Eric told me one day. "I just want to be friendly."

I still struggled with insomnia most nights. My psychiatrist gave me sleeping medication, but I worried it would make me too groggy the next day. At first, I refused to try it, instead spending my evenings making phone calls to any friend who would pick up and listen to my pity party.

Poor Susan got the brunt of it. I'd call her in the middle of the night and unload all my anxieties, resentment and questions about how to navigate life as a single mother. She never complained once, God bless her. I tried not to call too often, knowing she had a husband and her own small children to care for, but I desperately needed some guidance.

There were nights when none of my friends answered the phone, leaving me to face the loneliness I feared so much. Anxiety crawled all over my body on those nights and sometimes birthed into sheer panic. Everybody kept saying they were proud of me and the way I'd built a life for myself and the boys. The reality was I'd never lived without another adult taking care of things.

If there had been a handbook on how to function in the world alone, I would have added it to my mounting self-help book collection. My heart was an open festering hole that I filled up with unhealthy coping skills, like a full liquor cabinet and a credit card with a $10,000 limit.

My drinking increased in the days leading up to Christmas. All the boys' presents arrived on time, and I sipped on rum and

Coke as I wrapped each one and put it under our beautiful tree. Eric's stepfather, Don, had taken us to pick out a Douglas Fir the week before. Eric and I had already agreed that he would have the boys on Christmas Eve to take them to his parents' house for their annual holiday party. It was the first time I wouldn't be invited since I was sixteen years old. The idea of missing it hurt like hell.

Eric's parents and I avoided talking about the party for weeks, hurt by the knowledge they couldn't include me and I couldn't accept. I wouldn't see Don dress up like Santa Claus in his authentic-looking red suit for the little kids. He always played the part beautifully. Even the children in the immediate family didn't know it was really their Papa until they got older and were in on the secret.

There would be no peanut butter cookies, no barbecued pork sandwiches, no twinkling lights strung along the back patio to gaze at. There would be no hugs and sweet words and little gifts for the only family I'd known since I was in high school.

Instead, Michelle would be at the party in my place. I let my mind drift there for a minute, imagining her picking up little Shawn to sit him on Santa/Papa's lap. I got a mental image of Michelle helping Brandon open the present from inside Santa's large red sack with the white fur trim. It felt like someone else was living my life, taking my spot as if I were interchangeable. Even more than losing Eric, losing his family was excruciating.

Christmas Eve finally arrived with Eric's car idling in my driveway. I steeled myself and let the boys run out the back door to greet him. When I followed them outside, I knelt down to their eye level and leaned over to hug Brandon. "Mommy loves you so much," I promised him. Then I picked up Shawn and held him close to my body long enough to smell his freshly washed hair. They both looked so handsome.

When I couldn't avoid it any longer, I looked at Eric with absolute fury on my face but refused to cry in front of him. I would be stoic and indifferent to him and his whole family.

I felt an odd choking sensation in the back of my throat. Before Eric pulled out of the driveway, I hurried inside and vomited in the downstairs bathroom. When I was finished, I looked out my kitchen window to find that Eric and the boys were gone. Running upstairs to my bedroom, I sobbed for what seemed like hours until my temples throbbed and my eyes burned.

When I screamed out into silence, the sound bounced off the walls and pierced my ears. I downed a whole bottle of wine in a way that wasn't the least bit social. *I was dead to them, the family I so loved.*

I reached for my unused bottle of sleeping pills on the nightstand. Maybe I could take one, pass out and forget everything that happened. The only problem was that I knew I'd wake up in the morning with the pain still fresh.

With my brain buzzing from the alcohol, I spilled the prescription bottle out onto my dresser and lined up the medication. I took one pill, then took another. The same thought tumbled around in my head as I swallowed. *Nobody needs me anymore.* The more I considered it, the stronger I believed it. I took another pill with a deep breath. *Everyone would be better off if I didn't exist. I was a terrible wife, and now I'm a terrible mother.*

My heart was broken and my spirit disintegrated. I knew I was thinking through a fog of depression, but it all seemed to make perfect sense.

Letting my tears flow freely, I put the rest of the pills in my mouth and chased them with what was left of my wine until they were all gone.

Chapter Six

I awoke with a fuzzy malfunctioning brain and no idea what day or time it was. My eyes wouldn't open all the way just yet, but I heard intermittent beeping noises, feet shuffling past me and random bits of conversation. When I became fully alert, I realized I was in the hospital. A stern-looking lady in nurses' scrubs was standing over me.

"Take this," she instructed as she thrust a small cup of charcoal liquid toward my face. "If you don't, we'll have to use the tube. Drink it all."

I drank it all. It tasted like a chalkboard, but the thought of any sort of tube near me was scary.

The nurse stood and considered me for a moment. "You could have died," she said bluntly. I tried to think of something to say that would indicate I thought this was a bad thing, but words escaped me. Everything I said kept coming out all jumbled anyway.

The nurse informed me that I showed up to the hospital in my car and collapsed in the waiting room. *Wait, I drove myself here? I could have killed myself.* The irony was not lost on me, but I felt ashamed at the thought I also could have killed another person. All I remembered was a quick image of the road, a stop light ahead, a panic attack and the first signs of dizziness. Maybe it was better that my mind couldn't fill in all the blanks just yet.

"When will I be discharged"? I asked hopefully, thinking that nothing sounded better at that moment than lying under the 800 thread count sheets I'd bought on my used and abused credit card. Maybe I'd watch some Sex and the City on DVD to take my mind off things for a while and dull the pain I felt.

"You won't be," the nurse answered. "After you're done here, you're going to a psychiatric hospital. It's the law for attempted suicide, and there's no way to get around it." *Did she just smirk? What a great bedside manner.* It occurred to me that I was being harsh. My nurse probably dealt with life and death all day long. The thought of some middle-class suburban lady squandering her precious life away just had to piss her off. I totally understood.

My hospital stay lasted about 24 hours before I was deemed physically stable for discharge. Mental stability was obviously another story. I wondered what the psychiatric hospital would be like. I'd seen old movies where people ended up in mental hospitals and suffered abuse either at the hands of the staff or by their fellow patients. My whole body was awash in terror at the thought of it.

Nobody came to visit me while I was in the hospital. I didn't call anyone either, but I was sure the news was out by now that I'd fallen apart and had some sort of breakdown. I thought of my boys, probably for the first time since they drove away with Eric on Christmas Eve. The thought of killing myself and leaving them motherless dug a pain in my chest that was sharp and relentless. I'd been so selfish taking those sleeping pills, and I wished I could somehow take it back.

As the hospital was getting ready for my discharge, a police officer appeared in the doorway to drive me to the mental hospital. Tears sprang to my eyes when I saw him take out his handcuffs. He seemed almost embarrassed as he explained it was protocol. It felt like my lowest point so far. The officer then approached me, smiled and then put the handcuffs back on his belt.

"It's all right," he said kindly. "We can make an exception. I don't think you're going to cause any trouble."

It was the first nice thing anyone had said to me in an entire day. We walked together out to his patrol car, the sudden appearance of the bright sun piercing my eyes. I still wasn't feeling well, but it was probably a good sign that I was glad to be out of my hospital bed. Sitting in the back seat, I kept my eye on the policeman through the Plexiglas that separated us. He turned around to look at me.

"Are you okay?"

I lied and nodded my head yes before realizing he was just asking if I was comfortable. Leaning my head back against the seat, I closed my eyes for the rest of the trip.

If the lobby was any indication, the psychiatric hospital was going to be like staying at a hotel. The walls were bathed in soft pinks, and the room itself seemed almost classy. A flat-screen TV sat in the corner playing the home shopping channel. The sound was off as if it didn't want to trigger the other patients. The officer wished me good luck and left me by myself.

I sat shaking in my chair until my name was called. A professional-looking woman directed me to a small office where a man was waiting. He seemed somewhat agitated as he asked me to tell the story of why I would try to kill myself. I sat calmly and unfolded the last few months for him through a fresh set of tears.

The intake guy sighed and looked down at his papers before he spoke. "You know," he said, "I don't really like your husband."

I had no idea how to answer that. It was true that I didn't like Eric either, but the right words from him would still have given me hope of putting our family back together. Was that love? I didn't know anymore.

The man doing the intake decided that I would go into the "less dangerous" unit, mostly people with attempted suicides and depression.   It scared me to think of what the dangerous unit might be like, and I thanked him for his help.

"Of course," he answered as he led me down a poorly lit hallway.   "A little lady like you would get chewed up and spit out in there."

The unit was nothing like the lobby had been.   Everything was minimal and stark, painted an ugly green color that looked like vomit and gave the rooms a strange glowing hue. My first concern was about all the people. They were everywhere, patients and staff, yelling at each other across the nurses' station, grabbing something to eat from a snack cart, crying so loudly I thought it had to be faked for the nurses' benefit. Some of them even screamed. My sensations instantly became overloaded.

One of the unit nurses showed me to my room and locked the door behind us. She asked for my purse so she could go through it looking for contraband. I was grateful to see the empty bed next to mine. *Thank God, I don't have a roommate.* The nurse ordered me into the bathroom to put on a gown so she could do an exam. I was too tired to fight about it. She searched me up and down everywhere and then let me get dressed again. "Get some rest," she said in a gruff voice.

I settled down on the hospital bed, far from home and from my boys and wishing I could talk to them. As my body hit the off switch, I realized it was still Christmas Day. That reality was still too painful to deal with, so I pushed the thought aside and shut down into an uneven sleep.

"Who are you? What are you doing in this room"? A woman's voice shocked me awake. She sounded more curious than angry, but her shrill tone hurt my aching head.

I opened my eyes to see a young wiry lady in a hospital gown standing at the foot of my bed. A nurse was arranging her things on the other side of the room. I couldn't tell what time it was, but outside the sky was dark. The patient in front of me seemed hyperactive and out of control. She leaned nosily over to look at me like she was trying to figure me out. She then let forth a rambling speech of word salad that was impossible to keep up with. I had no idea what she was talking about.

"This is Annie," the nurse explained as she continued to unpack. "She's going to be your roommate."

I tried to smile at Annie politely, which seemed to charge her up even more. She asked me personal questions like where I lived and how old I was, but she didn't wait for an answer before she talked over me at a scary rapid pace. Hospital gowns being what they were, she also exposed herself several times without knowing it, but I had enough respect to look away.

"Annie is manic right now," the nurse whispered. "Don't worry, her medication will kick in soon." She then made a hasty escape back to the nurses' station, where I imagined she would read a fashion magazine with her coworkers in total peace and quiet. I suddenly hated her.

Annie probably took a pause of breath every five minutes, and when she did I leaned back and closed my eyes and prayed for her to go away. While she was rambling, I tried to coo and sympathize and do anything I could think of to make her stop talking. I already envisioned her attacking me in a fury for not answering one of her repetitive questions. Finally, about the fifth time she woke me up, I looked up at her in tears. "I'm so tired," I whined. Annie patted my head and clucked in understanding. She continued talking until the sun came up, then promptly passed out in her own bed.

I saw my psychiatric doctor later that morning. By then, my main focus was checking out of the mental hospital through any means necessary. I tried my best to look "normal" as I sat across from the doctor and told him how much I regretted trying to kill myself, swearing to God I would never do such a terrible thing again.

The gravity of what I could have done to myself and the boys had already begun to smother me. I felt like the most selfish person on Earth, but I forced a smile at the doctor and told him that I was certainly well enough to leave. The doctor explained that according to the law I had to stay a minimum of 48 hours, so I spent the rest of the day sitting as close as possible to the nurses' station, deathly afraid one of the other patients would hurt me.

The unit was loud and raucous, and I constantly scanned the patients making the most noise to see if they were about to get violent. Unfortunately, it didn't cross my mind that I was just as sick as they were.

Some were depressed and some manic, but none of them were any different from me. *If I could just get out of here,* I reasoned. *I'd*

be able to think clearly and sleep and start to put
my life back together.

The doctor finally released me the next day. I called Eric's mother from the hospital after realizing I had no car and no way to get home. Elaine showed up about an hour later with a big hug and assured me that everything was going to be all right. Maybe she'd been telling the truth that I would always be her daughter.

I leaned into her and cried quietly, the weight of the last few days lifted by her touch and kind words. She had been a mother to me since I was sixteen years old. She was involved in just about every aspect of my life. It hurt to know deep down I was probably kidding myself, but I felt safe and relaxed as she drove me to her house to see the boys.

The boys! How could I ever face them after what I'd done? Brandon was only seven and Shawn almost three. It could have scarred Brandon for life, and Shawn would have had only fleeting memories of me as he got older. When I walked through the front door of Elaine's and Don's house, I felt my throat swell and my eyes get watery. It wasn't the mother I wanted them to see. For them I could be strong, if not for myself. The boys came running, both yelling "Mom" with excitement, and crashed into my arms with hugs and giggles. It was more than I deserved, but I still let myself bask in it.

Eric showed up to the house later when the boys and I were playing catch in Elaine's backyard. I spontaneously hugged him out of the gratefulness of being alive and the thought that he actually cared about that. He only had one question, "Why?"

I thought about telling him my truth, that the whole thing was his fault for having a stupid affair with his stupid receptionist and throwing away fifteen years of marriage like it was a crushed soda can. I wanted to tell him I hated his guts for the aloofness he treated me with afterward, brushing me off so his new girlfriend didn't get her nose out of joint. Then there was the casual way he picked up the boys with Michelle in the car until I demanded he stop. He must have known he was ripping my heart out every single time.

I didn't say any of those things to Eric though. Instead, I mumbled something about going through a hard time. He asked me if I thought I was well enough to care for the boys. I saw where the conversation was going and quickly defended myself. Those boys were my lifeline. Eric taking them to live with him and his mistress would have been the cherry on top of the last six horrible months. He seemed a little relieved as I insisted I was fine and ready to take the boys right back to my house.

Taking Brandon and Shawn home with me wasn't exactly the plan yet. I still needed to reassure Elaine that I'd be okay, but my determination was enough to make Eric go away. I hated him for not being devastated at the thought of losing me forever, but I was already long gone to him. Watching him leave, for the first time I began to harden my heart when it came to Eric. Once the boys and I headed home in the backseat of Elaine's car, I remembered the two of them were all that really mattered. I put an arm around each of them and squeezed tight. My

children were with me, and I'd never let
anything come between us again. Their little
faces made life seem full of possibility and
hope that all three of us would be fine.

Chapter Seven

Loneliness always waited in the shadows, biding its time until it was ready to pounce again. It saturated my bones and made me sick from the inside out. I was a flower planted in dirt, desperate for even the tiniest drop of water. A continuous loop played in my head of Eric and Michelle cuddling on their couch watching TV together and having Sunday dinners at Elaine and Don's. The mental images hurt so much more than any sexual act the two of them could have engaged in.

I was running out of people to listen to my troubles. Everyone grew weary of me complaining all the time. My friends all had their own spouses and homes to worry about. I drank way too much rum and Coke at dinner and didn't stop until I was stumbling drunk. It made me ashamed when the boys had to shake me awake to put them to bed.

Being the world's biggest loser was a full-time job except for the sliver of happiness every morning when I woke up, before I remembered. I'd spend the rest of the day submerged in the pain of standing still while life went on without me.

Boundaries in my life were becoming more scarce. I signed up for online dating way before I had any business doing it. My first intention was to make Eric jealous and remind him of what he was missing. I created a lackluster profile, not knowing how to tell men about myself. It's hard to explain yourself when you don't know who you are. I went on a couple of dates, but I ran like hell when any man wanted to get closer physically or emotionally. The thought of another man touching me almost made me ill.

I spun up a platonic friendship with a man named Micah on Plenty of Fish. We hadn't met in person but liked the same bands, including Depeche Mode and Bauhaus.

Reading his dating profile, I realized that Micah was five years younger than me. His picture made him look like a "goth" with spiky blond hair, black leather pants, combat boots, no shirt and a nonexistent tan despite living in Florida. I wasn't interested in dating him, but I thought he seemed sort of edgy and cool. It surprised me how much we had in common despite looking like total opposites. He made me feel interesting when I chatted with him, even though I was the living definition of "not" cool.

After a few weeks of writing back and forth, Micah asked if I wanted to meet him to shoot pool at a bar near his house. I said yes, not considering it a date but merely hanging out as friends. Micah would never be interested in somebody like me, a boring soccer mom with a recent ugly divorce. Even so, I liked playing pool and was usually pretty good at it.

Micah asked me if I would pick him up at his place because his car wasn't working. I paused for a moment. My other "dates" were always in public places for safety reasons. Micah seemed okay, but how would I really know? Maybe I could pick him up and stay outside and wait in the car for him. My need to connect with another person and have some fun outweighed any potential red flags

I could be missing.

A few days later, I followed Micah's directions and pulled up in front of a rundown mobile home in a questionable part of town. There were no lights on inside, and I wondered if Micah had stood me up or sent me to the wrong place. I'd just made the decision to drive away when the front door swung open and a voice called my name.

"Hey Glenna, I'll be out in a few minutes, okay"?

I shouted okay back, unable to catch a glimpse of Micah. What was taking him so long to get ready? I spotted an eviction notice hanging in his front window and suddenly felt embarrassed for him. Even in the dark, his trailer looked almost dilapidated from the outside. I wondered whether the inside was worse or better than the outside.

Part of me wanted to put my car in reverse and leave, but I didn't want to insult him or be judgmental. I'd never shame someone based on where they lived, and I wouldn't do that to Micah when he'd been so nice to me.

The trailer door opened again about twenty minutes later.

"Hey, you wanna come inside for a minute"? Micah called out.

I reached for my car's door handle and hesitated. It didn't seem like the safest situation in the world, but Micah was waiting and I didn't want to insult him. *I will scream and run at the first sign of trouble,* I assured myself as I walked up the rickety makeshift stairs and through the front door. It was pitch black inside, but I saw a tiny flash of red as Micah put a cigarette out from across the room.

"Ugh, these gross things," he groaned. "I only smoke them once in a while. I'd quit for you though."

It was an odd comment considering we had just met, but I brushed it away like everything else that evening. I sat on the couch as Micah walked around the trailer turning on various lights. Suddenly, I understood why he spent his time in the dark. Junk filled every corner of the living room, probably to cover up the gaping holes in the floor. Cords and cables were strewn everywhere with wires that led back outside. I assumed it was an attempt to rig up illegal electricity or cable, but I didn't ask.

Peeking around the corner, I noticed a toilet smack in the middle of the master bedroom. There were no walls around it and no door, just a random toilet sitting there all by itself.

In the midst of the disarray, I noticed a small black cat darting back and forth. Micah picked it up and dropped it in my lap.

"She's pregnant," he announced. "Feel her belly, it's *life!*"

Micah smiled at me as I pet his cat. She smelled a little musty like the trailer itself, but Micah's words gave her the weight of importance.

Micah took the kitty back and reached out an arm toward me. "You ready to go shoot pool?" he asked.

I finally got a good look at him in the light. He was of average height and weight and had bleached blond hair. There was a large colorful tattoo on his right arm. He wore a black concert T-shirt and ripped jeans. His face was covered in caked-on foundation with eyeliner outlining the rims of his eyes like he'd just stepped out of an 1980's Ratt video. He told me online that he was 32, but he dressed like he was 15. *No judgment*, I decided as I followed him back to my car.

Micah and I drove around the corner and up the street to his favorite pool hall where he ordered us drinks. I made sure I paid for them to clarify we weren't on a date. It might be bad if he got the wrong idea. Sitting at the bar side by side, we chatted long enough to order two more rounds.

Micah beat me at pool twice, taking turns playing and then sitting back at the bar to drink more. I paid for every round, sensing that money was tight for him. We talked about his parents and my divorce and former family and our jobs. Micah said he worked for his best friend's lawn service during the week. I wondered whether he made enough money to take care of his eviction problem, but I didn't want to pry.

Micah told me he grew up as a Jehovah's Witness. His family went to the Kingdom Hall every week, and all the people they associated with were also Jehovah's Witnesses. He told me how bummed he was every Christmas when the school kids had their new toys and he had nothing. He said he used to sneak downstairs at night to watch A Charlie Brown Christmas and Frosty The Snowman since they were forbidden in his home.

He then confided that he was caught smoking pot when he was sixteen and became disfellowshipped by his own community. I tried to imagine what it would be like, everyone he knew turning their heads away on sight and never speaking to him again. It seemed cruel to do to a kid, and

I felt compassion for Micah going through it.

When it was time to leave, we walked out onto the sidewalk together. Micah playfully spun me around underneath a street light as if trying to get a better look. "I have to say," he told me, "you're much more attractive in person." I smiled and let the compliment soak through the agony in my heart. It seemed like forever since somebody treated me so kindly.

Dropping him off at the trailer, I wondered if Micah would try to kiss me. Instead he gave me a friendly hug and got out of the car. *He is a gentleman,* I convinced myself as I pulled out of the gravel driveway.

Even if I never saw Micah again, for one night I felt attractive and important. It was something to hold me over. Not only did I get through the "friend date" unscathed, I actually felt a little bit better about myself. I decided it was definitely worth the risk.

Chapter Eight

After the night we played pool, Micah
called me no less than five times a day. The
conversations were brief, just him saying
how much he liked me and how cute he
thought I was. He told me he had a great
time the other night and couldn't wait to see
me again. I collected the compliments like
wildflowers, each one of them causing my
self-esteem to bloom a little more.

When I told my best friends about Micah, I
conveniently left out his living situation and
the five-year age difference along with other
concerns that were getting harder to ignore. I
wanted my friends to be happy for me, to see
I was worthy of love and that everything
would be okay. My life had come full circle,
and I believed Eric tossing me aside was just
making room for something better.

I hired babysitters a few nights a week to
spend more time at the trailer. Micah cooked
me elaborate gourmet dinners that were a
pleasant surprise each time. I ate on his

couch with him watching me expectantly for a response, and I made sure to gush about the food. It was awkward being stared at while I ate, but it seemed important to Micah. We watched stolen cable TV through the wires running across the floor. It seemed wrong, but who was I to ask questions?

Micah still smoked cigarettes despite offering to quit for me. When we drank together, I'd bum a few and smoke them myself. It had been almost 20 years since I smoked back in high school, but my addiction picked up right where it had left off. Soon, I was buying my own packs and sharing them with Micah.

Some nights we listened to music after dinner. Although we had similar tastes, I soon learned he also loved 80's hair metal. He admitted his favorite band was Motley Crue, which he proved by once answering the door with thick black streaks of eyeliner under his eyes like Nikki Sixx. I laughed at the cheesy lyrics about fast cars and fast women, not realizing how much Micah took them to heart.

It didn't take long to figure out that Micah drank a lot. Once I went into his kitchen to ask if he needed help making dinner. He was crouched near the sink drinking straight from the bottle of vodka I'd brought over. Sometimes Micah's boss would give him a little nugget of pot that he shared with me. I hadn't smoked marijuana since the eleventh grade and didn't remember liking it all that much, but I went with the flow and smoked it with him. Being stoned made it easy to forget my troubles and relax for a change.

It crossed my mind how much Eric would disapprove of me drinking and getting high. He didn't let me have so much as a glass of wine during all our years together. It almost felt like every vodka shot and every toke I took with Micah was a middle finger pointing straight up at my ex-husband. It felt quite liberating. The experience reminded me of when I was a free-spirited teenager before Eric took me under his wing. He was as much a parent as a partner, and I'd never questioned him once throughout our whole marriage. Now, I was questioning everything.

Things began to change with Micah after a couple of months. His calls became less frequent, and he sounded irritated while we were talking. It wasn't automatic anymore that he would invite me over to the trailer on nights that Eric had the boys.

Confused, I tried to figure out what I had done wrong. I'd tried to keep things light with him because he said he wasn't interested in anything serious. Could I have backed off *too* much? I missed the constant contact we'd been having and the sweet things he would say. They always lifted my mood, and I felt starved for air when Micah took his attention away.

He called one afternoon out of nowhere to ask me a favor. He said he needed to check his email, but he didn't have access to a computer because the library was closed. He wanted to give me his password so I could check and see if he had messages. I agreed to help, but after I hung up I realized I had a virtual gold mine in my hands. I knew Micah had Facebook and wondered if the password was the same as for his email. Maybe if I looked at his account, I'd find a clue why he was blowing me off. I'd never hacked anybody before in my life and knew it was wrong, but I was desperate for answers. *It's for my own self-protection,* I reasoned. Micah and I were hardly in love, but I didn't think I could stand another blow to my badly wounded heart. Was he chatting with somebody else? Did he chat with a friend about me? I needed to find out what was going on.

The passwords turned out to be the same, so I logged into Micah's Facebook and started checking his private messages. They were mostly from other women who looked like Gothic vampires with pale skin covered in tattoos. As I read further, I discovered Micah was pursuing each woman to sleep with him. There was one woman in particular who he seemed interested in, and their messages were filled with sexual jokes and innuendos. I felt creepy reading the messages, but unfortunately I discovered what I'd been most worried about yet prayed not to find.

I'm fucking this MILF lately, so I've been getting a lot of action, Micah wrote. *You know*

how those divorced women are. They can't get
enough. It's not that I like her all that much, but
she gets huge alimony from her ex-husband.

My heart broke on the spot, and I shut the
computer off without reading any more. I
meant nothing to Micah. All the nice things
he said were complete bullshit so he could
get laid or get money or whatever else he
thought he could weasel out of me. Those
pictures of women who looked and acted
like the exact opposite of me made me feel
jealous and stupid. I swore I would never
speak to Micah again and do my best to
forget him. It shouldn't be that hard to forget
some lame guy with a drinking problem and
serious immaturity issues.

I was ready for Micah's call a few days
later. When it finally came, I stuck to my
resolve not to answer the phone, forgetting
he had the habit of calling back every five
minutes until I picked up. I tried to shut my
phone off, but when I turned it back on my
voicemail was full of messages from him to
call right away. I'd have to do it the hard
way. The next time he called, I answered the
phone.

Micah sounded close to hysterical. He explained that his wall unit air conditioner had broken down, and he didn't have the $200 to pay for a new one. It was the beginning of summer with the Florida sun already harsh and unforgiving. He wanted to know if I could help him out if he paid me back.

I wanted to hang up on him without saying one word. I wanted to yell into the speaker that I'd seen his awful messages and knew the sad truth about him. Instead, I picked him up and took him to buy the air conditioner. It wasn't in my nature to let anybody suffer, even at my own expense. Besides, I couldn't go back to life the way it was when nobody wanted me. I knew Micah didn't really want me either, but his kind words as I drove him back to his trailer after we bought the wall unit were still capable of melting my heart.

My plan was to drop him and his air conditioner off and drive away forever. Instead, he invited me to come inside. *One last time won't matter.* I promised myself I'd still dump him, but what could be the harm in one night just to say goodbye? At least I knew what the deal was and wasn't in the dark anymore.

Micah shared his bottle of vodka with me. I drank more than usual, trying to cover up how livid I was. I swore I wouldn't sleep with him that night, but he made short work of that boundary and took me to his bed.

"Even though I'm not ready to say it, I think I love you," Micah said as we fell asleep.

It was the first time he'd ever said those words. Granted, he said it through a heavy filter of liquor, but I still swooned over them. Of course, I couldn't trust that he actually loved me, but part of me wanted to bask in it anyway and pretend it was true.

The next morning, I tried to play it cool. Micah greeted me with a smile and hugged me tight. I didn't bring up what he had said the night before about loving me, fearful he would take it back. He asked if I could drop him off at the library so he could use their computer. When I took my time getting ready to leave, he became more urgent about it and asked me to hurry up.

When I dropped Micah off, he hugged me goodbye and disappeared inside the building. He didn't make plans to see me again and didn't say when or if he would call. I told myself it was okay if he never contacted me again. It was supposed to be our last night together, but my brain and heart battled in a tug-of-war that neither could win.

Waiting for Eric to bring Brandon and Shawn home from his house, I felt guilty about how little time I'd been spending with the boys. I promised myself I would make it up to them and stop focusing on Micah. It was like I'd been in a fog for the past couple of months, and I knew I needed to get my head straight again. From now on, I would only drink on special occasions, not every day like before. It was important to be present for Brandon and Shawn now more than ever.

I couldn't figure Micah out, being so sweet

the night before and then pushing me out
the door in the morning. He was probably on
Facebook flirting with more women. The
thought made me sick to my stomach. Even
after saying I wouldn't go back and snoop, I
still had his password and the curiosity was
just too much. Before I knew it, I was looking
at his messages again. There were a few to
the girl he'd singled out before. She looked
like a lot of the other women he wrote to
with long dark hair and colorful tattoos
covering her scantily-clad body.

Micah wrote, *I kicked out the 36-year-old so
you could come over. What time can you get
here? I can't wait to see you.*

Bile rose in my throat. What was I doing
with a person like this? Micah and I were
never officially serious, but it grossed me out
that he could say he loved me one day, kick
me to the curb the next and then invite
somebody else over to sleep with him. Micah
was a total pig, and I would never speak to
him again. He could call as much as he
wanted, but I would not pick up the phone
or answer his emails.

I felt humiliated to be crying over such a complete jerk. Shutting off the computer, I got in bed and took a nap until the boys came home, thoroughly exhausted from lack of sleep. If I didn't take care of myself, I'd wind up with another depressive episode. I couldn't afford to let that happen again.

I stuck to my resolve not to talk to Micah. He messaged and called and wanted to know what was going on. Even though I didn't respond, his words already held power over me. It wasn't long before he was saying sweet things again, trying to get back in my good graces. I ached to hear him talk like that, for anybody to say those things to me. The isolation I faced without him was too much to bear. I never had plans anymore and nobody that cared for me. The thought of being alone for the rest of my life seemed terrifying.

You are strong, I reminded myself. *You have dealt with a lot worse than this punk and have come out even tougher than before.* I gave myself pep talks several times a day when the phone would ring, determined to wipe Micah from my memory forever.

Of course, being strong would have been a lot easier if I could remember when I'd had my last period.

Chapter Nine

A home pregnancy test the next day confirmed my fears. I was pregnant with Micah's baby. The test was just a formality as far as I was concerned. There was no way I could have another baby, especially with Micah as the father. The plus sign popped up on the test immediately after my first splash of urine, so I knew there was no mistake.

I felt like an idiot for not paying better attention to my cycle and the periods I'd missed. My symptoms of the recent need for daily naps and the mood swings should have been more clues. What kind of woman doesn't even take care of her own body?

Two days later, a sullen Micah went with me to the gynecologist. It seemed like the last place he wanted to be. He didn't say much when I shared the news with him. He definitely didn't smile and hug me either. I could tell he was disappointed. Being in the same boat, I understood how he felt.

A nurse gestured for me to get on the scale. "Oh," she said sweetly. "Your little baby belly is so cute."

I burst into tears on the spot. The nurse looked puzzled as she led me to the ultrasound lab where the doctor was waiting.

Avoiding Micah's eyes, I entered the lab and got up on the table. He was sitting in the corner of the darkened room. I couldn't see his facial expression, but I felt reasonably certain he was miserable. Part of me wished I never told him I was pregnant and dealt with it myself, but it didn't seem fair to keep the secret.

"I have to ask," Micah finally said. "Are you sure it's mine"? They weren't exactly the words that every pregnant woman wants to hear.

"There hasn't been anybody else," I assured him.

I told Micah he wasn't obligated to come

to the doctor with me, but I gave him credit for showing up. It must have taken him at least two buses to get to the office. It didn't really matter though. Having another baby at my age and in my situation seemed impossible. I simply wanted to put this mistake behind me and move on.

When the doctor arrived, I noticed she was young and very attractive. I imagined Micah checking her out as I lay on the table looking at the ceiling. My whole body shivered as the doctor rubbed cold gel on my belly. I would rather have been anyone else at that moment. When the ultrasound began, I turned my head toward the monitor and waited for the doctor to say something.

"Okay, well it looks like you're in your second trimester."

What? I felt like one of those women in tabloid articles who doesn't know she's pregnant until the baby drops out. How could I already be at least three months pregnant?

"Everything looks good from what I can

see here," the doctor continued. "Do you want to know the sex?"

My God! The baby had a sex already! This was real! I felt like one of those after-school specials in real life. Taking a deep breath, I slowly exhaled and nodded my head yes.

"It's a girl."

My heart melted as I started crying. The baby was no longer a situation; she was a she. Micah rose from his chair and came over to inspect the monitor. "A girl," he whispered loud enough for me to hear. The fetus was clearly formed on the monitor with a tiny baby outline with arms and legs moving back and forth.

In that moment, I knew I couldn't go through with the termination. Maybe I had no business bringing another child into my messed up life, but I owed it to this little girl to do the responsible thing and take care of her.

I was still crying when Micah and I left the office. He didn't say a word and instead lit up a cigarette, looking down at the sidewalk.

"I'm not going through with the abortion," I said quietly. "She's already a little person."

Micah nodded his head as if he'd known I would say it. He probably felt tricked into the whole thing, but at that point it didn't matter. She was my little girl. I was ready to have her without him, if needed. Even if I didn't feel attached yet to the life inside me, I knew she deserved a chance.

Micah walked toward the bus stop, then hesitated and turned around.

"You know," he called out. "We could take care of this baby together. I mean, get married and everything."

My jaw dropped in shock. I'd only known Micah for a few months. During that time, he'd made me cry as often as he'd made me smile. He was almost a baby himself, not in age but in attitude. He was about to be evicted from a trailer that should have been condemned long ago. Micah could barely take care of himself. Now he wanted to take care of me and our daughter?

"Don't worry," I said as he walked back over. "This isn't your problem. You didn't ask for this."

"Neither did you," Micah answered, "but the fact is there's a baby on the way and we need to figure things out. I want to marry you. You've been so good to me. You would be great with a little girl. I think we should try to make it work."

I glanced down at the ground and caught sight of Micah's shoes. They were both untied with the laces dragging the sidewalk, and I noticed his socks were two different colors. This man who could barely dress himself was offering to change everything in his life and marry me and raise our daughter. Why was I listening to a word he said?

Was it true that people could change? Could Micah actually step up and take care of things? Maybe I was selling him short all this time. I imagined him living in my beautiful yet lonely townhouse, helping with the boys and the new baby. The thought made me feel less alone. Who was I to judge Micah, especially after making such a colossal mistake myself by accidentally getting pregnant?

I knew how it felt to have parents that were never married. My own birth was the result of an affair between my parents, and I'd heard the word "bastard" whispered a few times when I was a young girl. I didn't want that for my daughter. It wasn't fair to her. She might find out and feel ashamed, and I would never want that kind of burden for any child.

"Let me think about it," I finally said. "We can talk more later."

Micah hugged me and hurried off to catch his bus. I felt bewildered as I drove home. The thought of telling people about the pregnancy made me nauseated, especially when I thought about the boys. Would they be upset with me? Surely they would tell their dad about it, as if my burgeoning belly wasn't enough of a giveaway. The thought of Eric knowing about the baby scared me, but part of me almost wanted to shove it in his face. *See, I've moved on without you. Somebody else wants to marry me and doesn't think I'm worthless and easy to discard.* The idea satisfied me.

When I got home, the phone was ringing. I thought it would be Micah. Maybe he changed his mind and wanted to dump me.

"Hello?"

"Oh hi, Glenna sweetie, my name is Darlene," an excited voice said back. "I'm Micah's mother."

I wondered how she got my number. We'd never spoken before, and I thought Micah was estranged from his parents.

Darlene kept talking. "I HAD to call you right away," she insisted. "I'm SO excited to have you as my new daughter-in-law. I'm SO happy for you and my son and the new life you're bringing into this world. When will the wedding take place? I hope it's SOON!"

Whoa, this was surreal. I hadn't even said anything close to a yes to Micah's proposal, and he's already calling his family? What was he thinking? Micah's mother kept chatting about the "wonderful" news. I was polite in return, but I wanted to hang up and call Micah to find out what the hell was going on.

"Well, I have to go," Darlene chirped. "I wanted to let you know how THRILLED I am that Micah has found a good woman like you."

I thanked her and hung up, then dialed Micah's number.

"You told your mom we're getting married?" My moment of politeness had passed.

"Well, yeah," Micah answered. "I mean, I know you didn't exactly say yes yet, but I could tell earlier that you're going to say yes."

"Really?"

"Come on," Micah nagged. He crooned over the phone like an R&B singer. "Baby, please don't leave meeeeeee."

I couldn't help but laugh for the first time in days. Before we hung up, I agreed to marry him.

Chapter Ten

"I think you're making a big mistake."

I rolled my eyes although Eric couldn't see me from the other end of the phone. He was the last person I wanted to talk to, but I knew it was necessary for Brandon and Shawn's sakes. I was hoping we could come up with a plan to share the baby news with them. Instead, Eric was calling my daughter a mistake as if I should agree and magically take it all back.

"Is this guy going to take care of you?"

Like you did? I didn't say it out loud. Even after fifteen years and a nasty divorce, I was still afraid to stand up to Eric. He'd always treated me more like a child than a partner. Still, I was getting tired of keeping things peaceful with him. Keeping the peace makes you shrink and leaves you wishing you said those unspoken words when it's too late.

"He will," I reassured Eric. I wished I were as confident as I sounded.

I didn't tell Eric about my upcoming wedding. It seemed like too much information for a single phone call. The news that Micah was moving in with us was going to be hard enough to share. Brandon and Shawn had only met him a handful of times when Micah stopped by the townhouse. They knew him as mom's "boyfriend." Brandon told his Grandma Elaine that he thought Micah was "cool." For his part, Micah never showed much interest in my boys. Now he would live with us as my husband.

Eric hung up without offering a solution for what to tell the boys. A few days later, I sat Brandon and Shawn down on the living room couch and tried to spin the news positively.

"Do I have to call him Dad?" Brandon asked. He bit his lower lip in concern. Brandon was just like me in so many ways. He was my worrier, my sensitive child.

"No, you already have a dad." I smiled at him and patted his back while he exhaled his deep breath.

Little Shawn chimed in, "Can I still go into your bed if I wake up in the middle of the night"? It was one of his favorite things to do. More often than not I would go to sleep alone and wake up to find his head on my pillow right next to me.

"Well," I answered truthfully. "I'm not sure, but you can always come get me if you need me at night."

Brandon smiled bravely, "I'm happy for you, Mom. It will be great. We get a new sister to play with." God bless him for trying to comfort me when he was the one who needed it more. That was Brandon's way. He'd gone through so many changes with the divorce, but even at the tender age of seven he was my rock.

Micah and I eloped to Las Vegas a few weeks later. I paid for the entire trip with my nearly maxed-out credit card. We got married in a small church that stood between an adult video store and a strip club. Our photographer promised to angle the pictures so those buildings wouldn't show. Micah wore a black tuxedo with a blue polka-dot vest and tie he picked out because it was what Nikki Sixx wore for the cover of the Theater of Pain album. I wore a barely off-white dress that did its best to cover up my growing midsection. I paid for both outfits.

Micah looked serious as he said his vows. He'd really been trying lately. He was being nice to the boys and loving with Jasper the dog, and he cooked for us almost every night. The boys became big fans of his homemade garlic bread. I felt like I was part of a family again. It didn't matter what Eric or anybody else thought. Maybe things would work out this time and I'd get my happily ever after.

Eric attempted to be nice to Micah when he picked up the boys and dropped them off. They shook hands, but when Micah turned away I saw disapproval on Eric's face. He thought Micah was weird with the spiky hair and tattoo. I shot Eric a dirty look in response. Sure, Micah wasn't conventional, but Eric had no right to judge my husband.

Who did he think he was?

I'd had no cigarettes or alcohol since my
ultrasound. The thought of the amount I
drank before I knew I was pregnant worried
me. Micah still brought home vodka on a
regular basis, but it didn't tempt me at all. I
only had four months of pregnancy to go.
Surely I could do without for the sake of my
unborn daughter. I hoped Micah would at
least tone his drinking down, but he drank
excessively every night as usual. When he
was drunk, he was loud and played his hair
metal music at full blast. The boys
complained about it, especially Brandon
with his sensitive ears. Micah ignored my
pleas to turn it down every time.

"I'm just having fun," he announced. "So
what if the kids don't like it?"

Our honeymoon period lasted only a few
weeks. Micah seemed to get frustrated more
often and wasn't shy about letting me know
it. One of his biggest irritations was Jasper.
Try as I might, the dog wasn't fully trained
yet and growing bigger by the second. The
boys adored him. Jasper would watch them

play video games in the living room and jump into their laps to give out kisses. He was the sweetest animal in the world, but Micah didn't like the barking or the dog poop he found on the floor or the way the dog rolled in the grass outside and got himself dirty. He wanted Jasper to spend more time in his training crate where he couldn't get in trouble.

I couldn't argue with the fact that Jasper needed more training. He wasn't doing well with going outside to do his business. Still, it seemed unfair to leave the poor thing locked up all day. I let him out during the day when Micah was at his landscaping job. The minute he came home from work, he insisted Jasper return to his crate.

I tried harder to train the dog and get him on a schedule. Jasper acted more nervous with Micah around, so I worked with him when Micah wasn't home. Nothing seemed to help though. The boys were miserable every time I put Jasper in his crate. Finally, I looked up a professional dog trainer on the Internet. The service sounded too good to be true. They would take Jasper for two weeks and bring him back to us fully trained. I hoped it would be a good solution. Underneath it all, I was grateful for the temporary peace in the house when Jasper was picked up. The boys were sad and missed him, but they were excited that he would come home and be a "good dog."

Micah's frustration extended to my boys as well. He complained that they were picky eaters. He said they didn't listen to him and that I was raising them to be "mama's boys." He became jealous of them and the time they took away from his wants and needs. Brandon and Shawn always had access to my bedroom, but now Micah slammed the door and told them loudly to go away. I defended the boys as much as I could, reminding myself that we were a blended family now. There were sure to be growing pains now that everything was different.

The tension kept escalating in the house. Brandon kept the peace by steering clear of Micah altogether. Shawn was more vocal about his displeasure. Whenever Micah tried to push his weight around, Shawn piped up in his little boy voice, "I don't like you, Micah." Micah was furious when I didn't correct Shawn for saying it, but I refused to punish my son for standing up for himself. Sometimes I disliked Micah, too, although I kept it to myself.

Being sober for a whole month was an eye opener. I wondered if I had only thought Micah was fun through a fog of alcohol and/or marijuana. He didn't really make silly jokes anymore. I didn't laugh when he sang and danced like he was manic to his favorite songs. Still, I wanted to make things work bad enough to push it all aside.

I tried to be generous with him, letting him use my car and my cell phone on days he had to work. During the weeknights, Micah didn't come home until late and was always more than a little tipsy. It shocked me when I opened my phone bill with a charge of nearly a thousand dollars for cellular data. When I confronted Micah, he claimed he didn't know he was being charged. I paid the bill with my credit card, but I didn't take my phone back. With all the time he spent out of the house, surely he needed it for emergencies more than I did. At the same time, I wondered who he spent so much time on the phone with that cost me a thousand dollars.

One Saturday afternoon in October, the boys and I were waiting at the kids' table in the lobby of Jupiter Auto Wash while the car was getting an oil change. I gave Brandon and Shawn some crayons and blank pages to scribble on as I colored and listened to them chatter happily. They were so sweet and fun to spend time with. I vowed to give them more attention even if it upset Micah.

I'd just finished coloring my paper when I felt a warm gush from below. *Did I just pee myself?* I stood up to go to the bathroom and felt a second gush. Hurrying into the ladies room, I locked the door behind me. My sweat pants were soaked with clear liquid that definitely wasn't urine. When trying to dry myself off with paper towels, more liquid came out and I was soaked all over again. My breath became shallow with panic at the thought something was wrong with the baby. I was only six months pregnant. It was way too soon.

I peeked my head out the door to check on the boys and found an older lady waiting for me. She said she was keeping an eye on Brandon and Shawn while I was in the bathroom.

"Are you okay"? Her face was wrinkled with concern.

"Yeah. I mean, not really. I'm not sure what's happening." I wondered if I looked as helpless as I felt. "I'm pregnant."

The lady called out to her husband to look after the boys for a minute and followed me into the bathroom. "I think your water broke," she warned.

"That can't be possible! I'm only six months pregnant. It's not time yet."

The woman walked me back out to the lobby, having grabbed a handful of paper towels from the counter. She led me to the nearest chair. "Don't move, stay as still as you can," she instructed. Brandon looked up from his coloring and saw me across the room. He was at my side in an instant. "Mom, what's wrong?"

"I'm not sure, honey, but there's nothing to worry about. I feel just fine." We both knew it was a lie.

An ambulance arrived a short time later. The paramedics quickly placed me onto a stretcher and told me to stay perfectly still. I needed a phone! The nice lady who helped me gave me hers to use. I called around until I finally reached Elaine and asked her to come and pick up the boys. The paramedics wanted to rush me to the hospital, but I couldn't leave until Brandon and Shawn were safe.

I was still lying on the stretcher when Elaine arrived a short time later. She squeezed my hand, and I burst into tears both for my baby and for the mother-in-law I'd lost. I needed a mom so badly.

"It will be all right," Elaine promised. "Sometimes nature takes its course and we find out later it was all for the best."

I thought about Elaine's words as they put me in the ambulance. My little girl deserved a chance. I'd already bought her some dresses and decorated her new bedroom in pink and yellow with glow-in-the-dark stars on the ceiling. Everyone around me talked about the baby only as a mistake I'd made, but she was as loved and wanted as if I'd planned for her. On the drive to the hospital, I prayed for both of us, fearful that we would never meet and I would never hold her in my arms.

Chapter Eleven

Once I reached the emergency room, the nurses flocked around me and chatted to each other in hushed voices. One of them put a slip of purple paper under me and announced that my water had broken. I was in active labor at six months pregnant. The urgency in her voice made me tremble with anxiety.

"What does that mean?" I demanded to know. "Do I have to go home on bed rest?" I couldn't imagine how that would even be possible with two boys, a husband, a dog and a job to worry about.

"You can't go anywhere," the nurse said, still with the wet paper in her hand.

"For how long?"

"You don't understand," the nurse informed me. "You have to stay here on bed rest until you deliver. You're at six months, so there's a chance the baby won't survive, but we're gonna start an IV and give you medicine to stop your labor and hope that will work."

I tried to calm my racing mind as they wheeled me upstairs. My daughter wasn't due for three months. I couldn't stay in the hospital for that long, unable to move, shower or even go to the bathroom. I was told I had to lie perfectly still at all times, but at that moment I wanted to leap right out of my skin. This couldn't be happening! I knew the boys were okay at Grandma's house, but what would happen to them if I wasn't home?

I shuddered at the thought of them going back to the townhouse with Micah, knowing he had neither the desire nor the capability to take care of them. Jasper was also due to come home the next day from the trainers. I didn't fool myself that Micah would have the patience with the dog no matter how well-trained he was. The need to make fast decisions overwhelmed me even as the nurses were telling me to relax.

Thankfully, my hospital room was private

and fairly large. The nurse told me I was on the same floor as other mothers trying equally hard not to have their babies too early. Those women were lying flat in bed just like me. I wasn't sure if it made me feel better or worse. The nurse hooked me up to a monitor that would track any contractions I was having. Even though I felt nothing, she informed me I was actually having them quite often.

After the nurse was finished, I called Micah. He'd already heard the news through Elaine, who asked him whether she could come by and pick up the boys' clothes. I breathed a huge sigh of relief that Brandon and Shawn were being taken care of by Eric and his family. It was one less thing I would have to worry about. Micah told me that Elaine had agreed to take him to the auto shop to pick up my car, and then he would drive over to the hospital. As much as my feelings for Micah were mixed up, I was grateful that I would have somebody to sit with me.

Micah showed up in my room later that evening with a giant bag of supplies. He'd cooked a pork roast at home and brought it with him to share with me, not that I was in any mood to eat. He grabbed my remote and turned on NFL football, excited that we could eat and watch it together as if we were at home. I was happy for the distraction and took a few bites and complimented Micah on his cooking. He was busy yelling at the TV with the game not going the way he wanted. When the nurse came to check on me, I apologized for the noise and assured her that everything was okay.

The next morning, I called the dog training company to ask if there was any way Jasper could stay for another week or two. I didn't know how long I'd be in the hospital, but at least I could buy my sweet dog extra time. The most the trainer would promise me was two extra days. I thanked him gratefully. Any amount of time was better than nothing.

I wondered where the boys were. Eric should have brought them to see me by now. I wanted them to know everything was okay after the scary experience at the auto shop. The nurses checked on me often to see if I was still having strong contractions, which thankfully were calming down with the medicine they were giving me. I had ultrasounds that showed my amniotic fluid too low for the baby, but my doctor told me she was all right otherwise. The rest of the time I spent by myself, thinking and praying and staying still as much as I could. My anxiety was so high I couldn't turn on the TV to distract myself. I missed being at home with the boys so much. It felt like I couldn't spend another 24 hours in the hospital much less the possible three months it would take to carry the baby to full term.

About a week into my stay, Micah called me sounding panicked. He said the dog training company had dropped off Jasper at the house, stating that they couldn't keep him any longer. My heart pounded wildly as Micah explained how Jasper had come home wearing an electric shock collar. The trainers handed Micah a remote and showed him how to use it and then left. *What the hell had they done to my dog?* None of the staff said one word about shocking our beloved pet when I signed up for training, or I would have never let him go.

"He's all freaked out," Micah complained. "What am I supposed to do with him"?

I was heartbroken by the abuse that Jasper had gone through, but I was helpless and stuck in a hospital bed. Through tears, I asked Micah to do the best he could and comfort the dog as much as possible. I would rather have a dog who made a few accidents on the carpet than see him suffer ever again. Yet again, I felt like everything was out of control. The boys needed me, my daughter needed me and now Jasper. When I hung up with Micah, I cried even harder. Maybe I was feeling sorry for myself, but the whole situation seemed unfair.

Eric called me the next day. I immediately plied him for information about Brandon and Shawn. He admitted he didn't think it was a good idea to bring them over to see me because the sight of me stuck in bed might upset them. I tried to argue, but I already knew I couldn't force him. Maybe Eric was right about it being too much for them. My heart ached to get home as soon as possible.

"Here's a weird coincidence," Eric said,

changing the subject. "Michelle is two floors below you right now."

"Why?"

"Well, she's been having terrible headaches, and they did a CAT scan and found some kind of tumor. They don't know yet whether it's benign or cancerous."

"Wow."

It was all the sympathy I could muster for the girl who had helped break up my marriage. Sure, a brain tumor was a big deal, but I already had enough on my plate without worrying about Michelle, too. Maybe it was insensitive, but she wasn't my problem anymore.

Micah rang my room constantly over the next week, yelling at the staff in the nurses' station if my line was busy. The nurses passed the messages along with a mixture of pity and annoyance, and I apologized on Micah's behalf several times. He never had much to say other than how Jasper was being a pain in the ass and asking when the doctors would let me go home.

As more time passed in the hospital, I became increasingly depressed. I had trouble eating and barely spoke a word to anybody, including the nurses. My hair hadn't been washed since my arrival. No friends or family were coming to visit me other than Micah. My heart was breaking for my boys. Without my knowledge, my obstetrician called a psychiatrist to evaluate me.

As I lay there in bed talking to the doctor about my situation, tears filled my eyes as I assured him everything was fine other than the pregnancy complications. He didn't seem to believe a word I said, but what good would it do to complain? No doctors could help me anyway unless they had a time machine.

On the same day I saw the psychiatrist, Micah called me all excited over some deal he'd found for music equipment. "It's everything I need if my friends and I do this band thing. I wouldn't even have to pay for it right away. They only want forty dollars a month until it's paid off, no interest or anything. Anyway, you know my credit's not great. They said I need somebody to cosign for me. Can you find out the fax number at the nurses' station so I can send you the papers to fill out?"

I barely understood what he was talking about. How was I supposed to be interested in music equipment and a stupid payment plan? Micah begged me to sign the papers, saying how great it would be to have a musical house and serenade me with his guitar. "I could do private concerts for you," he offered as if that were something I wanted. All I wanted was to have my daughter and go home, not that Micah had asked.

"Whatever, I have to go," I sighed. When the fax came in the next day, I gave in and signed the papers. What did it really matter? Every corner of my life was a shit show I didn't have the slightest idea how to clean up. Who cared if Micah wanted to buy a bunch of junk and pay for it monthly? I couldn't bring myself to care and grew tired of him pestering me about it.

Micah called back the next day, but not to thank me for the equipment. I heard him yelling through the phone, but I had trouble understanding what he was saying. Jasper was in the background barking loudly and aggressively. I'd never heard him bark like that before. Alarm bells went off in my head as I tried to put the story together.

"What's going on there?" My heart was pounding in my chest.

Micah was alternating between yelling at me and yelling at the dog. "Shut the fuck up! I came home from work and let Jasper out of the crate and he crapped all over the floor. What am I supposed to do with this animal? Get away from me, you stupid mutt! I had to shock him for doing it, but now he's freaking out."

"You did WHAT?"

"I shocked him like the trainer showed me. He kinda got scared, but then he barked all aggressively and came after me. Wait, hang on a second."

"No, Micah, YOU wait!"

I heard Jasper yelping in pain followed by a door slamming. My face flushed and my eyes were hot with angry tears. I was still yelling Micah's name when he came back to the phone.

"What did you DO?" I demanded. "Are you SHOCKING the dog?"

"Not that time," Micah explained. "I had to kick him to get him away from me. I thought he was going to attack me."

What the hell? I couldn't imagine Jasper attacking anybody ever. He was the sweetest young puppy I'd ever known. I got a mental image of Micah's combat boot contacting Jasper's sweet furry body and shuddered.

Micah continued talking, "I put him in the garage for now. He needs to just stay in there. What kind of dog craps himself two minutes after he gets out of his cage? I think something is wrong with him. Anyway..."

"No!" I stopped him. "Not anyway! Don't

119

you ever do that to my dog again. Throw the shock collar away. Do not touch him!" I gave the orders knowing I had no way to enforce them. With me stuck in the hospital, Micah was free to do whatever he wanted.

Not for long though, I reassured myself. When I got home, Micah was moving out, although he didn't know it yet. I never wanted to see his ugly face with an ugly heart to match ever again. He couldn't be trusted to take care of things, much less be present around my boys or even my dog. The decision practically made itself; he had to get out of our lives permanently.

Chapter Twelve

During my third week in the hospital, I
woke up one morning with steady cramps. I
called the nurse, who looked at the monitor
and assured me I wasn't having contractions.
She said I should try to relax; however, as
the morning progressed, the cramps hurt a
little more and seemed as if they were
coming and going regularly. I prayed the
nurse was right. It was only my 27th week of
pregnancy. When the doctor looked at my
ultrasound the day before, he said the baby
weighed less than two pounds. She needed
more time to grow and develop.

Still lying in bed, I suddenly felt
something shifting inside me and warmth
between my legs. I pulled back my blanket
to see if I'd soiled the bed. To my horror,
there was a tiny foot poking out of my
body. I panicked and called the nurse back
in. Her eyes widened when I showed her,
and she hurried to find a doctor.

Within minutes, the whole nursing staff
surrounded me. I didn't have time to say a

single word as they rushed me into an operating room. There wasn't time to call and let anybody know. The surgeon placed a mask over my face while nurses prepared me for a C-section. That was the last thing I remembered as the anesthesia took hold and I fell asleep.

When I woke up hours later, Micah was standing over me biting his lip.

"Glenna, wake up," he said impatiently as I drifted in and out of sleep.

"The baby," I struggled with the words, feeling unbelievably exhausted.

"She's alive," Micah informed me, "but they don't know if she'll make it. I saw her for a second. She's way too small."

The anesthesia finally wore off a short time later, and I recovered enough to transfer to a regular room. On the way there, the nurse promised she would wheel me past my daughter in the NICU so I could see her for a minute. I craned my neck and tried desperately to get a good look at her, but I couldn't sit up yet. Out of the corner of my eye, all I saw was a tiny incubator surrounded by doctors. Micah walked alongside the stretcher not saying a word. I understood how he felt. The whole thing was too much to process.

The baby's doctor arrived in my room a short time later. He explained that our daughter was right on the cusp at 27-1/2 weeks. Born any sooner, she would not have survived outside of the womb. The surgery had been difficult, and the doctor told me that as a result I could never carry another baby to full term again.

Before he left the room, the doctor warned me not to get my hopes up regarding the baby because things were touch and go. I ignored his advice. As long as there was hope, there was something I could hold on to. I fell back to sleep wishing I had gotten a better look at her.

When I woke up, Micah was still there, sitting in a chair next to the bed.

"We have to name her," I told him.

Micah frowned, "I thought we should probably wait, you know, just in case."

"Even if the worst happens," I argued, "she still needs a name. She's a real person, you know."

Micah brought me the suitcase I'd packed earlier, and I retrieved my baby naming book from inside. I honestly hadn't given a name much thought, thinking I still had a few months to come up with one. Together, Micah and I went through the book and named her Victoria. The name meant "victory," and I hoped it would help give her the strength to keep fighting.

Micah stayed in my room for the rest of the night and left for work in the morning. I was almost sad to see him leave. The combination of the traumatic experience and the morphine pumping inside me made me feel closer to him again. He promised to look in on Victoria on his way out of the hospital. It touched me he'd called her by her name. As angry as I was at him about Jasper, there was a part of me that still hoped he would change. Maybe his daughter would inspire him to turn over a new leaf. Faith had gotten me this far through the pregnancy and delivery. I still clung to it like a life raft.

Later in the day, my nurse came to walk me over to the NICU to see Victoria. I had trouble the day before even walking to the bathroom. My doctor ordered a blood transfusion to replace all I'd lost during surgery, and I felt a little better and stronger. The nurse kindly took my arm as we walked up to Victoria's incubator.

I finally got a good look at my daughter. She was barely visible underneath all the connected wires and tubes. Victoria looked so tiny and helpless in her incubator. The nurse explained that every day she lived increased the chances she would be all right. There was a hole inside the incubator with a glove attached. I put my hand through it and lightly petted Victoria's little back, afraid that I would accidentally jostle the tubing. Her eyes were closed, but she didn't appear to be in any pain.

"You are beautiful," I whispered to my daughter. "Mommy loves you."

My doctor discharged me from the hospital a few days later. It thrilled me to think of being with my boys again. I couldn't wait to go outside, to sleep in my own bed, to take a shower instead of a sponge bath. Still, I didn't want to leave Victoria in the hospital all by herself. She needed me there to talk to her and caress her and help her get through this ordeal. The doctor told me Victoria might be in the hospital until her actual birth date for a full-term infant. It was three months away, and I couldn't imagine waiting that long. I called Micah with mixed emotions and asked him to come pick me up.

"No, no, no!" His voice was urgent. "I'm not done yet. I have to get the house ready."

"Micah, I'm discharged. They won't let me hang out here."

"I'll be there later," Micah promised. "I have to get the house prepared."

Was he planning a surprise? What could he be talking about? I reminded him again that I had to leave right away. Didn't he realize how badly I wanted to get home? He sounded irritated as he promised to pick me up "as soon as possible."

Hours went by, and the staff grew impatient. "Isn't there somebody else who could come get you?" My nurse was nice but persistent. I tried to think of somebody I could depend on, then dialed the person I'd always depended on. Elaine picked up the phone on the first ring, and I explained my situation.

"Yes, I could come get you," she told me, "but what about your husband? Why can't he pick you up?"

"He won't do it." I said as I choked back tears. "I have no way to get home."

Elaine showed up a half an hour later. As we were leaving, I asked her if we could stop by the NICU so I could see Victoria. We stood side by side in front of the incubator, and out of nowhere Elaine squeezed my hand gently. "She's really a little fighter," she said.

I wished I could freeze the moment. Elaine was my mother again if only for a minute. I missed her terribly, and the familiar feeling of her hand in mine nearly wrecked me. We were quiet on the way to my townhouse, but I sincerely thanked her when we arrived. It felt good to be home.

Someone had left the back door unlocked. I didn't see my car in the driveway. Micah must have left without securing the house. I made a mental note to mention it when he got home from work. When I stepped inside, I immediately recoiled in shock, dropping my purse which slid to the floor with a thud. My entire townhouse was trashed. There was a loud angry bark coming from the living room.

I turned the corner to find Jasper trapped in his crate, so I hurried to let him out and comfort him. He looked much thinner with tangled fur into mats with the scent of a combination of urine, dirt and dog poop. The electric shock collar was still around his neck. Jasper licked my face as if to thank me as I removed it. Whatever ordeal I had been through, Jasper had also suffered. I sat with him quietly and petted him until I could no longer stand his smell.

Dishes were piled up in the sink. Plates of rotting food being munched on by fruit flies littered the rest of the kitchen. There were stains on the carpet that hadn't been there before I left. The floors were sticky and gross, and there was garbage and junk strewn throughout the whole living room.

I spotted a ton of brand new music equipment rising almost to the ceiling, including giant speakers and amps, Micah's guitar and a microphone with a stand. It looked like everything a band would take on a national tour. This was the stuff he'd "needed" so badly? It looked like a giant sore thumb in the middle of my once beautiful and immaculate townhouse.

My heart sank. My townhouse looked like Micah's shitty trailer. There was no way I'd ever get it all cleaned up, especially exhausted and in pain from my surgery. I wanted desperately to give Jasper a bath in the upstairs tub, but I didn't have the strength.

My anger grew greater the longer I stood there. Micah had ruined everything in my life I cared about. He clearly had to get out of my house, and when I got my energy back I planned to show him the door personally. I climbed upstairs and found that my bedroom matched the rest of the house with takeout wrappers everywhere and stains on my favorite burgundy comforter.

I was too tired to cry again, so I took one of the pain pills the doctor had given me and crawled into bed, falling asleep almost instantly with thoughts in my head of how I would break up with my husband.

Chapter Thirteen

It was dark outside when I finally woke up. I wanted to call the boys, but it seemed too late in the day. Eric was keeping them for an extra day or two while I recovered. When I sat up, a sharp pain shot across my pelvis. I put my hand down and felt the long horizontal scar that stretched across my skin.

Checking to make sure enough time had passed, I reached for another one of the pain pills. The bottle felt considerably lighter than when I'd gone to sleep. Maybe I was just imagining things. I couldn't be sure in my current state.

It surprised me to find Micah downstairs trying to clean the kitchen. He saw me standing there and greeted me with a huge grin.

"Hey," I said to him, "did you take…"

Micah interrupted my sentence and crossed the room to hug me so hard that I winced in pain. "I saw that you were home, but I wanted to let you sleep. Come here, sit down and listen to this."

While I sat on the couch, Micah messed with a bunch of cables and hooked up his amp and speakers.

"Micah, I don't feel well," I pleaded. "Can we do this later?"

"No, wait, only for a second, okay?" Micah insisted. "I want you to hear what this stuff can do."

The next few minutes were torture. Micah turned everything on and picked up his guitar. The noise he produced was nothing less than ear splitting. My whole house shook every time he played a note. He was usually half decent on the guitar, but all the stuff he was plugged into made him sound horrible. I wondered how much he'd been "practicing" with it and how often the neighbors had complained.

"The stupid bitch next door called the cops on me the other night," Micah said, reading my mind. "They didn't do shit, though. I turned it back on after they left."

"I'm sorry, Micah, but I really need to go back to bed. I'm super exhausted." I would have said anything to get him to stop.

I could tell it disappointed him, but he turned off the equipment and went back into the kitchen to clean. "I'm sorry the house looks so bad," he offered. "I've been working so much I haven't had time to clean." I found that hard to believe as it would have taken a lot of free time to get my townhouse in such a terrible condition. It was way beyond the bottle of 409 he was spraying all over the counters.

I nodded and went back upstairs. It was true that I was tired, but I also wanted to avoid Micah because I still planned to ask him to leave. I patted the side of my leg for Jasper to follow me upstairs in case Micah got the idea to play guitar again.

Two days later, when Micah was at work, I felt well enough to leave the house. My first stop was to see Victoria. The nurse gave me a chair to put next to her incubator, and I leaned down close to her little head. I talked to her like I used to talk to the boys when they were first born with loving sing-song words. Victoria was wonderful, a true miracle and a little fighter. I told her over and over how much I loved her. The nurse told me she was holding on steadily. I was grateful for the good news, but I hated to leave her by herself.

My next stop was the bank. I was still hurting and already worn out, but I went inside and withdrew one thousand dollars in cash. My plan was to give it to Micah as an incentive for him to move out. I decided that I would tell him that night when he got home.

Back at the house, I put the money on the kitchen counter and sat down in one of my wooden dining room chairs to wait. I wished I had something for my pain, but the pill bottle was already empty. I'd already guessed it was thanks to Micah. Since I got home from the hospital, I'd only taken a couple of pills when the pain was really bad. They shouldn't have disappeared so fast.

Just another reason Micah had to get out of my house.

I felt increasingly nervous as the hours grew later. What if he yelled at me? What if he tried to hurt me? Although he hadn't laid a hand on me before, part of me felt it was within the realm of possibility. I prayed that the money would keep him calm and he would just agree to go quietly, but the thought didn't stop my hands from shaking.

I was still in the same chair when Micah came home. "Hey," he said cheerfully. "You must feel better."

"Not really," I answered. "I'm in pain, but I have none of the pills left that the doctor gave me."

"Bummer," Micah looked sheepish. I could tell he wanted to change the subject, so I let it go. It was more important he take the cash and leave. I picked up the money and held it out to him with my hands still trembling.

"What's this?" Micah asked.

"It's one thousand dollars," I answered. Even my voice was shaking. "I… I want you to move out."

Micah gasped. It was clear he hadn't seen it coming. "Why? I mean, I don't get it."

I braced myself and stood up slowly, "I don't want to talk about anything or get into a bunch of reasons. I just think it would be better if you left."

Micah narrowed his dark brown eyes. "But you can't do that," he informed me. "I live here. I get mail here. That makes it legal on its own. You can't just throw me out."

I wasn't sure if he was telling the truth about the mail. Yes, mail had come to the house for him, but what rights did that give him? I mentally kicked myself for not checking things like that ahead of time.

"You've just been through a lot," Micah decided. "You're not thinking clearly. I know you don't want me to go. You don't want to be here all by yourself taking care of three kids and an uncontrollable dog. It's too much for you to handle."

He had a point. I could barely even make it up and down the stairs, much less wash the dog and feed the kids and give baths and all the other things they needed.

"I love you, Glenna." Micah reached out and held my hand, the one without the cash in it. "How are you ever going to find another man in your condition and with three kids to boot? That doesn't exactly make you a catch, I'm just saying."

I was too tired to feel insulted. "It's not always going to be like this," I said. "I'll get better and be able to take care of things by myself."

"You don't have to though," Micah reasoned. "I'm here. I'm Victoria's father. Doesn't that count for something?"

He was confusing me. The strength I thought I had to kick him out vanished. Maybe parts of what he was saying were right. He also wasn't taking the big chunk of money I was offering. Didn't that mean something?

"Let me think about it," I finally said to buy myself some time. "I have to lie down."

"Yes," Micah agreed. "Go up to bed. When you wake up, I'll make you dinner. Then we can talk more."

I felt defeated as I climbed the stairs. Brandon and Shawn were coming home the next morning. Even though I was happy about that, I knew there wouldn't be much time to rest and recover. I needed to preserve my energy for their arrival. First I put Micah's money back in my purse, and then I crawled into bed and fell asleep. *There's still time*, I promised myself as I drifted off. *I'll feel better soon, and then Micah really has to leave for good.*

Chapter Fourteen

Eric brought the boys home the next day, and my heart sang when I laid eyes on their sweet little faces. It felt like forever since we'd been together. I swore I would never let so much time pass with us apart ever again. Eric stood in the doorway, waiting for me to invite him in. It was the last thing I wanted to do considering the state of my home. I'd cleaned up as much as I could, but it still looked horrible. I knew he would judge me for it.

"What's wrong with Jasper," Brandon asked, pointing to the dog in his crate. Eric subtly peeked his head into the living room and looked around, his expression speaking volumes of how disappointed he was in me.

"Nothing is wrong with him, honey," I reassured Brandon. "He just needs a bath. I haven't had a chance to give him one."

Shawn piped up, "Why can't he come out of his crate?"

139

"Of course, he can come out," I undid the latch so Jasper could rain kisses on both the boys. As dirty and smelly as he was, the boys petted him lovingly, and the dog ate up the attention.

"Can I talk to you"? Eric was in my living room now. *Damn it!*

We went back outside. I stood with my arms folded, waiting for Eric to blast me. I already felt guilty enough about Jasper, and I knew he was about to pile on.

"You have to do something about that dog. He can't just live in a cage like that."

I couldn't tell him I wasn't letting Jasper out because I was afraid Micah would hurt him again. I was afraid it would lead to truth after truth about my new husband's behavior, which was none of Eric's business other than regarding the boys. He still thought of me as a child, just like during our marriage for all those years. It was his nature to speak to me like I was a kid. I knew I couldn't mention to Eric how I'd tried to pay off Micah to leave. I'm sure he would have told me to kick him out for free and never look back.

"What's all that shit in the living room?" Eric was referring to Micah's music equipment. I couldn't explain that I had the same question. What would the boys think if Micah ever played it in the house again, especially Brandon who got upset by loud noises?

"Everything is fine," I assured Eric. "I just got home from the hospital and still need to organize everything, but it won't happen overnight. I need a little time."

Eric looked thoroughly unsatisfied by my explanation, but he said goodbye to the boys and left. I was grateful that Micah was at work. The boys and I sat on the couch, and they filled me in on everything they'd been doing for the past few weeks. We talked about Pokemon and school and their friends and how Victoria was doing in the hospital and anything other than the messy house and messy dog.

"Can we go see Victoria?" Shawn asked.

I told him I was visiting her every day I could, but that he and Brandon were too young to be in the NICU. I offered to bring pictures and letters to the hospital to get them involved, but it wasn't the same and we all knew it. It must have been so confusing to them to hear I was having a baby, only to come home from the hospital by myself without her and no idea when she could join our family.

Micah came home later that evening. I quickly put Jasper back into the crate. The boys were playing quietly upstairs in the room they shared.

"Oh, they're here"? Micah pointed to the suitcases on the couch. I nodded yes. He went straight upstairs to hibernate in the master bedroom.

Over the next few days, I tried to come up with a plan to end things with Micah, although halfheartedly. The thought of another broken marriage and divorce was depressing, not to mention the guilt of separating him from his new daughter. He'd been nice around the house lately, charming and funny again. He went back to making dinners for all of us. I suspected he was trying to find a way back on my good side, and I had to admit it was working.

Also in the back of my mind was the nagging seed that Micah had planted. What if he was right that I couldn't handle things all by myself? I thought about my breakup with Eric and how depressed I'd been, staying in bed and crying for months on end. The boys didn't need to go through that again.

It was clear from the last time I tried that Micah wouldn't go easily. I still didn't know if his claim about receiving mail making him a legal resident was true. Part of me wondered if I should just go with the flow for a while, especially with Micah on his best behavior. Was it true that people could change? Maybe the feelings he had for me and the baby could turn his life around.

I wished I still had a friend or two that would talk to me. Most of the people I considered my friends backed off from me after I married Micah. They also didn't hesitate to tell me I was making a terrible mistake. I reasoned that the majority didn't really even know him, not like I did, and they were basing their decisions on things I told them. Maybe I shouldn't have vented so much about the bad times, because now it seemed unfair to Micah.

I visited Victoria in the hospital every day and encouraged Micah to do the same. He told me he wanted to try to go to the hospital after work. I still wasn't able to touch or hold my child, but I still went nearly every day. I'd pull up a chair and sit next to her, whispering sweet nothings as close as I could get to her ear. The doctors called her a fighter and said although she originally had the slimmest chance of living, the chances for her grew greater every day. She was truly a little miracle.

Micah called up a few of his friends in the city to join his "band." One of his friends, Josh, had a music room set up in his house, so Micah hauled all his equipment over there where they practiced for hours. I said a prayer of gratitude that they weren't practicing in my townhouse. Micah told me they were looking for gigs, thinking that if people heard them just once, it would be his ticket to fame. I didn't have the heart to discourage him. He told me the name of the band was Anakim, which I guessed was a cool name he found somewhere on the Internet.

The band finally landed a show at a Miami club frequented by "goths" who dressed entirely in black, top to bottom. I drove down there with Micah, who was jumping out of his skin with excitement. He wore the full rock star outfit, ripped jeans and a concert T-shirt with spiky hair and thick black eyeliner. I'd gone all out and wore a pair of fishnet stockings with a short black dress and black boots. I felt a little ridiculous, but Micah assured me I was "super hot."

"I can't wait for you to take videos to show my parents," he said. "You know I come from a musical family. They're going to be so proud."

I couldn't help but get caught up in it. Micah seemed so happy, more than I'd ever seen him. He usually didn't get along with his parents, and I could tell he thought the video of him playing and singing on stage would bring them back around. After hearing about the dysfunction in the family from Micah, I wasn't sure whether that was good or bad.

Micah and the band set up in a room near the back of the club. Another band was already playing up front to a packed audience. People started to gather around us looking curious, and Micah greeted them all with the promise that it would be an amazing show.

After they were introduced by the manager, Anakim started with their first song. The music sounded fuzzy and depressing, and I could barely understand what Micah was singing. People started to move back to the front of the club to hear the other band instead.

Anakim only played three songs to a handful of people. I worried Micah would be upset about the weak turnout, but after the show he ran up to me and hugged me.

"Wasn't that awesome? Did I sound good? You got video, right?"

I nodded my head yes to all his questions. If Micah had a great night, that was all that mattered. I waited while he packed up, and we made the long drive home with Micah chatting the whole way about what an amazing night it had been. He was almost childlike in his enthusiasm.

The next day, I edited the video I took of the band. Micah asked me to send it to his mother's email address. He was really proud of it and sure his parents would love to see it. He was like a little boy eager to please his mom and dad. I could tell it was important to him to get back into their good graces.

Micah's mother emailed back later that afternoon.

I can't believe my own son would do something so evil! Even the name of the band is satanic! You are an APOSTATE, and we want nothing to do with you!

"What's an apostate?" I asked Micah.

"It's like the worst thing you can call somebody as a Jehovah's Witness. She thinks I'm as bad as Satan."

Micah was crushed. He tried writing his mom back, but he was too hurt and angry. When he cried, I held him in my arms and told him it was okay.

"We'll be your family," I promised him. He leaned his head against me and shut his eyes as if he were home.

Chapter Fifteen

The peace in the townhouse lasted about a month, the downward spiral beginning when Shawn was feeling a little hyper one Saturday night. He ran like a banshee back and forth across the upstairs hallway, laughing and shouting and letting off steam before bed. The noise was enough to bring Micah out of our bedroom and yell at my boy to stop. Shawn halted for a second, and suddenly his happy energy turned to furious anger.

"I HATE you, Micah," Shawn shouted at the top of his lungs. It shocked me to hear the venom in my little guy's voice. He was usually so easygoing. Shawn ran into his room and slammed the door hard.

"Aren't you going to do anything?" Micah was incredulous. "You can't let him talk to your husband that way. Go in there and punish him."

I went into Shawn's room, but I had no

intention of following Micah's orders.

"What's the matter, baby?" I asked my son, who was standing in the middle of the room with his fists balled up tight.

"I hate his guts," Shawn said loudly enough for Micah to hear in the hallway. "I wish I could kill him!"

His reaction startled me. Why did he feel so much hate for his new stepfather? Was he jealous of me spending more time with Micah than I had with him lately? Micah came bursting into the room, and it dismayed me to see the same look of hate in his eyes. Were they jealous of each other?

"Spank him!" Micah demanded.

Shawn's eyes widened in surprise. I had never spanked the boys in my life and always considered corporal punishment an excuse for lazy parenting. It only seemed to teach children that it was okay to hit when you're angry.

Shawn crossed the room and tried to push

Micah out. Micah scooped him up and walked with him down the hall into the spare bedroom where it was dark. He set Shawn down and shut the door behind him, the little boy screaming. "NO!"

Shawn opened the door and tried to come out, but Micah turned him around and put him back in and shut the door again. This time, he gripped the door handle so Shawn couldn't escape. My son went from screaming to crying hysterically. I pushed Micah away and let Shawn out of the room. He was crying and shaking, and I held him as close as I could in a full-body hug.

"Ugh," Micah said in disgust, walking back down the hallway and disappearing into the other bedroom. I stayed with Shawn until he calmed down enough to go to bed next to Brandon, who had thankfully stayed out of sight during the ordeal. *At least Micah hadn't hit Shawn*, I kept telling myself. It didn't make me feel much better.

"Why would you do that to a four-year-old?" I asked Micah as I stormed into our bedroom. "He's scared to death right now."

"Oh, come on," Micah protested. "I barely even touched him. Does he look bruised to you?"

"It doesn't matter. He's still really upset. I could barely get him to bed."

"Hey," Micah said. "I know I'm not their father and don't make decisions here, but stop coddling those boys. They will grow up to be sissies. Look at them. They go to Boy Scouts for Christ's sake. That's not something a cool kid would do. He's gonna get bullied, and you better do something about it now before it gets worse."

I didn't know where all this came from. Micah hadn't spent a lot of time with the boys one on one, but he'd never insulted them before. Sure, I questioned my parenting skills regularly, but I always tried to raise the boys from the heart and with love. Now that was a bad thing?

The spiral continued after the weekend was over. I got an angry email all in capital letters from Eric, who had the boys at his house overnight.

"WOULD YOU MIND TELLING ME HOW BRANDON GOT SHOT WITH A PELLET GUN AT YOUR HOUSE?"

My first thought was that Eric was trying to start trouble. I had no guns in the house, pellet or otherwise. Brandon hadn't said one word about getting shot by Micah. I picked up the phone and called Eric directly to ask him what he was talking about.

"He told me Micah shot him with a pellet gun, Glenna. There's an ugly red mark on his leg. You didn't see it?"

"No, Brandon never showed it to me or said a word," I answered as tears formed in my eyes. *What the hell?*

"I don't know how I feel about Micah being around my kids," Eric confessed. "I mean, I know he's your husband and all."

"Wait," I stopped him. Then I told him the truth, all of it. Well, except the part where I'd been drinking so much. Could I have been drunk or passed out when this happened to Brandon? I wasn't sure, but I kept that detail to myself. I spilled everything else though, including the wrecked townhouse, Jasper, the music equipment and how I tried to get Micah to leave and failed.

"Well," Eric said after I finished, "if Micah won't leave, then I think you have to do it."

It was something I'd never considered, packing up the kids and moving out of the townhouse. After Micah "redecorated" the whole place, I didn't really feel attached to it anymore. I wasn't proud of it the way I used to be, not to mention that I was three months behind on paying the mortgage. The last time I paid it I used my credit card.

I wasn't able to work or make the amount needed to keep up because I'd been in the hospital for so long. Truth be told, I had also worked little since I'd been home. My anxiety was too great every day to sit down in front of my computer and transcribe. I barely had any money left, except in credit, and I didn't know how I would pay that off either.

I confessed all this to Eric. He stunned me by offering to pay for the boys and I to get a new place with first month's rent and a deposit. He said he would keep the boys until I found a place and wanted to pay for a hotel room where I could be safe until then.

I was thankful, yet still scared. Micah wouldn't let me go so easily. I'd have to pack up and leave while he was at work. It was better if he didn't know my whereabouts so he couldn't constantly call and show up and bother me. The new plan was forming in my head. I shared it with Eric who agreed and told me "the sooner, the better."

Eric was a lifesaver. We weren't in love anymore, but it was clear enough that he still cared. I gratefully accepted his offer of help and assured him it was over with Micah for good, even though I wasn't yet sure if I believed it.

Chapter Sixteen

The boys and I moved into a small duplex on the other side of town. There were three bedrooms, perfect for when Victoria finally came home. The boys even made new friends in the neighborhood as I was unpacking our stuff. We hadn't brought everything with us, time being of the essence, but we had grabbed most of the toys, books and games the kids loved so much.

Eric arranged for a moving company to help with the rest, but much of it got left behind in our haste to get out of the townhouse. I moved all in one day when Micah was at work. He was taking the bus every day to get home, not to mention the extra hours every day he spent riding his bike around the city with a pint of vodka, stopping to drink in various grocery store bathrooms. I knew we had plenty of time.

Eric advised me to cut off all contact with Micah. He worried that Micah had some psychological hold over me and that I would cave if I let him get close enough. I promised Eric that wouldn't be a problem. I blocked Micah on social media and changed my phone number; however, I left my email the same. I told myself it was just in case of an emergency, but truthfully I worried about how Micah would respond to us leaving. If I let him vent in emails and get all his anger out, I could delete them whenever they came in.

We still lived in the same city, and I worried about running into him somewhere. He knew I went to visit Victoria at the hospital every day, but he hadn't gone to see his daughter even one time since her birth. I felt relatively safe that wouldn't change.

The hardest part was Jasper. I couldn't bring him to the duplex with us as the landlord didn't allow dogs. I also wasn't confident about my ability to take care of him anymore. Sitting down with the boys, I explained everything, telling them Jasper needed a home where he would be loved and cared for. When they cried, I held them and dried their tears, telling them again how sorry I was. I was just as heartbroken as they were, so tired of letting my loved ones down.

I took Jasper by myself to a shelter the next day when the boys were at school. On the phone, the agency told me it was a no-kill shelter. I breathed a sigh of relief knowing Jasper would be okay, but I hoped he wouldn't be scared to be locked up in a cage with other dogs until somebody adopted him. The poor little guy had spent too much of his life in a cage already.

I loaded Jasper into my car and drove to the shelter with tears in my eyes. As I was filling out the paperwork at the front counter, I heard a woman's voice behind me.

"Is that your dog?" A woman with long dark hair was leaning down petting Jasper. I felt embarrassed as I realized he must smell horrible. His fur was still matted and tangled. Nodding my head, I explained in a trembling voice that I had to leave him at the shelter.

The woman considered Jasper for a

minute as she continued to pet him. The dog looked up at her with adoration and panted heavily, almost smiling back at her.

"My name is Cindy," the woman said. "I'd like to adopt him if that's okay with you."

It was better than okay. It made me happy that Cindy saw something special in Jasper. Under all that mess, he truly was a beautiful dog. She must have known it, too. We signed the papers, and I walked Jasper and his new owner out to her car. She even had a doggie seatbelt she gently strapped him into. I leaned over and petted my good boy and told him how sorry I was that I didn't do my best for him. By the time Cindy came back around to my side of the car, my eyes were filled with tears.

"I promise I'll take good care of him," Cindy said as she hugged me. She didn't have to tell me. I already knew.

We exchanged email addresses, and Cindy promised to send me pictures of Jasper as often as she could. She was an angel in disguise with her kind words and her

159

seatbelt for dogs. She cooed at Jasper as she shut the car door. I could tell she loved him already and would give him a peaceful life. It was all I'd ever wanted for him.

I did the best I could to make our new place a real home for Brandon and Shawn, going to Target so I could buy stuff to decorate with money I didn't have. The rent at the duplex was about half of what my mortgage had been, but I hadn't been paying the mortgage at the townhouse either. I'd always been terrible with budgeting. Eric always took care of stuff like that during our marriage. Since the age of sixteen, I'd let him be in control of all our money. That was when I thought he would never leave and I wouldn't ever have to learn how to manage anything on my own.

Eric stopped by to pick up the boys on his regular schedule, and he seemed pleased at how we'd settled in. I couldn't thank him enough for helping us. When we were alone for a minute, he gave me an update on his girlfriend's condition. Sadly, Michelle's brain tumor turned out to be malignant, and the cancer had spread all over her body and bones. The news shocked me. Michelle seemed way too young to be dealing with cancer. Even so, whenever I thought about her, I still felt hatred. I hid it from Eric and told him to let me know if they needed anything. Honestly, I didn't know what else to say. Eric said he was planning to tell the boys soon.

When Brandon and Shawn came home from their dad's, they followed me into my bedroom and stood next to each other at the foot of my bed looking sad and confused.

"Do you know Michelle is going to die?" Brandon asked.

"Yes I do," I answered quietly.

The boys looked at each other, then back at me. It was the first time I thought of the effect Michelle's death would have on them. She was always there on weekends when the boys were with their father. She'd played with them and cuddled them and gently teased them. Now she was about to disappear from their lives forever.

Brandon and Shawn had grown to like Michelle, and I knew the news would leave them upset and confused. My heart hurt at the thought of my children hurting. Death was hard enough even for adults to understand.

Shawn spoke next, "Is she going to be a beautiful angel in heaven? That's what Dad told us."

I swallowed my anger and sarcasm, and it tasted bitter on my tongue.

"Yes, she is," I told my son as he wriggled his way into my lap.

Both Brandon and Shawn were full of questions. Did Michelle have to die? Couldn't a doctor save her? What if we wished really hard? In their world, people didn't just go away forever. In their innocent eyes there was always hope. My heart broke to see them feeling so helpless.

I scooped up both boys in my arms. "Maybe we can do something to help Michelle feel better."

Their faces lit up as they followed me to the kitchen. I pulled out a wicker basket from the top shelf of the pantry and lined it with bright red tissue paper.

"Okay," I said. "What do you guys think would make her happy?"

"I know!" Shawn shouted. He ran off in the direction of his room and came back with a small stuffed monkey I'd given him. It was one of his favorites. He knelt down and set it into the basket tenderly. Then he stood up and turned back to me.

"What else?"

Brandon and Shawn each drew Michelle pictures that we stuffed into colorful envelopes. I put some unopened Clinique moisturizer I'd bought recently into the basket along with a small African Violet plant I'd halfheartedly been looking after. The boys added more stuffed animals until the basket was almost overflowing. They chatted happily about what Michelle would say when she got it and how surprised she

163

would be. Before we knew it, we were finished.

"Doesn't it need a card?" Brandon asked.

I grabbed a Sharpie and an index card. The boys hovered over me around the dining room table.

"What should we write?" I asked them.

"How about... get well soon?" Shawn offered.

I hugged my little boy. Neither of them really understood how final this was.

"How about... we love you, Michelle?" I suggested.

"Yeah!" both boys shouted in unison. Brandon wrote it down since Shawn couldn't spell yet, although he did add a smiley face. We stood over the basket in silence looking at our handiwork. There would be time to have a real talk with them about Michelle's death, but not in that moment. They were so excited about helping her. It was all that mattered for all three of us.

Eric seemed touched by the gesture when we presented the basket to him. He told me later that Michelle had been excited to get it before she passed. He said she was happier at the thought of a truce between us than anything I'd put in the basket. Even though I still didn't like her, I realized a lot of my anger was misdirected. I blamed Michelle for blowing up my marriage, but she wasn't the one who promised to be loyal. Eric made that promise on our wedding day, and in the end he was the one who broke it.

Chapter Seventeen

Micah's harassing emails started shortly
after we moved into the duplex. He was
heartbroken, aloof and borderline suicidal all
at the same time. Most of what he wrote was
about my unfairness after everything he'd
sacrificed to be with me. He wrote that the
thought of becoming homeless terrified him
once he got evicted from the townhouse.
What would happen to him then?

Micah was sorry for not being nicer to the
boys, but he promised he'd change if I'd give
him one more chance. He reminded me we
had a daughter together. Didn't that mean
anything? Did I want her to grow up
without a father?

I promised myself I wouldn't read his
messages, then promptly broke that promise
as soon as the first one arrived. In all of
them, he begged me to meet him one last
time and talk to him. I spent more time
worrying about Micah than my own
situation, which was that the rent was
coming due and I had no way of paying it.

Out of sheer stupidity and misplaced guilt, I agreed to meet Micah at the food court in our local mall. He looked thinner. I wondered if he had been eating. There were dark circles under his eyes as if he hadn't slept. I could tell he was drunk both by his behavior and the small vodka bottle I saw stashed in his pant leg. He excused himself to go to the bathroom several times, where I knew he'd be drinking even more.

"Please don't do this," Micah pleaded when he returned. "I know we went through some hard times, but I love you and I want to be with you. That's all I want. I can help you raise the baby. You don't have to do it all by yourself. I know Eric probably helped you out when you moved, but where is he now? Isn't he with his girlfriend? Who will be there for you? You don't have family around. I know you lost most of your friends because of me, but I'm still here and I want to help. We could be so happy."

It was everything I'd always wanted to hear him say, but I knew I couldn't give in. Eric would kill me after everything he'd done to help me, and my few remaining friends would likely do the same. At the same time, part of me didn't want to be alone and wanted somebody to love me and take care of me. Micah couldn't even take care of himself, but who else would want a woman in her late 30s with three kids from two different fathers? Here was Micah, looking at me so lovingly the way I'd always wanted. Was it love or fear that made him want me so much? The same question was true about my feelings for him.

I stood up from the table and stuck to my guns, telling Micah I wasn't coming back. He stood up and hugged me tight, pulling me in and wrapping his arms around me as if he never wanted to let go. He was trying to make me feel safe, and it almost worked. How safe would I be all alone?

Micah kept emailing after that, even though I sent back responses with only a word or two. He clearly felt we'd "shared a moment" at the mall and was more determined than ever to work things out. I had more pressing issues with the rent due shortly. Even though I'd transcribed extra hours, I still only had about half of what I needed. One Saturday morning, I hauled a bunch of furniture and other assorted items out to my front lawn and held an impromptu yard sale. Most of my stuff was still in good condition. I would have liked to keep it, but there was no time to be sentimental. The boys got excited and brought out some old toys they wanted to sell, and I let them keep the money they made.

Sometimes I felt restless. It seemed like forever since I'd been out anywhere. Drinking in the privacy of my bedroom wasn't fun at all. One night, after a few rum and Cokes, I did a search on Facebook to find some people that lived in the Jupiter area. I randomly sent friend requests to both men and women. It was time to make some new friends.

I received a message from a woman named Tricia. She wrote that it seemed strange for me to request her as a friend because she usually only got friend requests from men. When I explained that I was looking for some cool people to hang out with, Tricia's suspicious attitude changed. We made plans to meet up and maybe have lunch or dinner. The two of us chatted online in the days leading up to our meeting in person. I confided to her all about Micah and everything that happened between us. It was nice to have a sympathetic ear. Tricia and I decided to go out and have a few drinks to see if we would hit it off as friends. It was a little strange, almost like a date with a woman, but I was grateful to have a new buddy.

The night Tricia was supposed to pick me up soon arrived. The boys were spending the weekend with Eric, and I was more than ready to have some fun. I had a new dress for the occasion, borrowing from the rent money again. The dress was black and slinky, yet not too sleazy. My hair and makeup were both on point. As I was touching up my lipstick, I heard a knock at the door.

"Tricia," I called out. "You're early."

Micah stood in my doorway. "I'm sorry," he said, crying hard. "I couldn't take it anymore."

Against my better judgment, I let him come in and sat him down on the couch. He continued to weep as he told me he felt the walls at the townhouse were closing in on him. He said he saw me in every corner of every room. He sobbed that he felt like he was going crazy and shouldn't be alone. He said he was suicidal.

"How did you find my place?" I asked him.

"It doesn't matter," he answered, waving his hand in front of my face. "I rode my bike from the townhouse just to see you. All I can think about is you. It's killing me…"

His words trailed off as he finally looked at me for the first time since he'd shown up.

"Are you going OUT?" he asked incredulously. "Where are you going? Who are you going with?"

I told him to relax. "I'm having a few drinks with a friend of mine."

"Don't go," he begged. "Stay here with me. Please, let's talk."

Tricia showed up at that moment. She was a heavyset blonde woman with a strikingly beautiful face and a warm smile when she gathered me up for a hug. I sensed her confusion by seeing Micah in my house after everything I'd said about him. Suddenly, I just wanted Micah to go away. He was a narcissist and would never hurt himself anyway. I had no time to sit and coddle him.

I introduced Micah to Tricia. They eyed each other suspiciously. Maybe I shouldn't have described him as "pure evil" in my messages to her.

"I have to go, Micah." I tried to be as direct as possible. "You have to leave so I can lock up."

Micah's jaw dropped. He was used to getting his way with me. Now I was disobeying him. "Thanks a lot," he muttered as he rode off on his bicycle. I apologized to Tricia, who said it was no problem and that she was just glad to see him go.

"He gives me the creeps," she announced. I didn't answer back, feeling strangely protective of Micah. He wasn't creepy. She didn't even know him.

Tricia and I went to a bar in the next town over. We got drunk in short order and ended up dancing with a group of random guys who were celebrating a birthday. Tricia and I hit it off fabulously as friends, and the night was a total blast.

I tried not to worry about Micah as I danced with one man and then another. Maybe it wasn't fair to him, but it was fun I believed I desperately needed. By the time Tricia drove me home, I could barely stumble up my driveway. Once inside, I crashed on the couch, hoping I wouldn't have to pay too high a price in the morning with my hangover. Even if I did, the little taste of freedom was worth it.

Chapter Eighteen

Micah showed up drunk at my bedroom's sliding glass door a few nights later. I frantically begged him to leave. The boys were in their beds sleeping, and it terrified me that they would wake up and see him.

"I can't go," he insisted. "I need to be with you."

It was out of the question. There was no way we could be together and especially not right then. I tried not to think of how long it had been since somebody touched me as I whispered no. It was a word Micah didn't understand. If there was a boundary, he bulldozed his way across it and kept going.

I only had so much strength to resist. A small part of me missed him, the man who could be so charming and make me laugh harder than anyone. There were good times, weren't there?

Micah took me in his arms, "Please let me stay," he murmured in my ear.

Just this once, what could it hurt? I would tell him after that he had to go before the boys woke up. It wasn't like the sex would mean anything, just two lonely souls looking for some temporary comfort. One time and then we could go back to being separated. I let myself melt under Micah, and for a little while I forgot I was alone.

"Mom," I heard the next morning. "What is Micah doing here?"

I shot up like a rocket to see Shawn standing in my doorway. Oh my God, I'd fallen asleep with Micah right next to me. I shook him awake.

"Get out of here now!"

"What?" Micah sat up in bed. "Why?"

"The boys saw you! I'm in enough trouble already. You have to leave."

"So what if they saw me?" Micah said huffily. "I'm your husband. I have every right to be with my wife."

175

Oh God, I realized that even though the night before changed nothing for me, in Micah's eyes we had reconciled. I felt bad, like I'd used him, but there was no time to think about that now.

"Seriously, just go!" I shouted. Micah disappeared out the back door with a hurt look on his face. I went into the boys' room, and Shawn jumped up to hug me while Brandon sat on his bed looking at the wall next to him.

"I'm not back together with Micah," I promised them. "He was just going through a hard time and needed somebody to talk to."

I could tell Brandon wasn't buying it. I'd promised him it was over and he would never have to see Micah again. I felt so selfish for putting my own needs in front of what the boys needed. Why did I even let Micah in the house? I could see the damage done in my children's sweet faces. Not to mention Micah, who I'd hurt as well. It was so inconsiderate and selfish of me.

Sure enough, the boys told their dad about Micah the next time he picked them up. I didn't ask them not to tell. It wouldn't have been fair to make them carry a burden like that. I prepared to face the music with Eric and withstand whatever anger he threw my way.

He was furious when he dropped Brandon and Shawn off. His look of disappointment killed me.

"What happened?" he asked. "You were doing so well."

"I still am," I assured him. "It was one time, and it will never happen again. I'm done."

I could tell Eric wanted to believe me, but he couldn't bring himself to do it. How could he feel comfortable about the boys living with me when I was making bad decisions and screwing up my life? I don't know if he realized that without the boys and Victoria there was nothing to keep me alive. Without them, I was mere seconds away from swallowing another bottle of pills or purposefully crashing my car into a tree. Eric left without saying another word. Maybe he sensed it more than I realized.

Once the boys were in school, I made my usual trek to the hospital to sit with Victoria for a while. I petted my daughter's back with a gloved hand and told her how much I loved her. Maybe I was ruining everything else in my life, but my little girl connected to endless tubes and wires helped put things in perspective. *This too shall pass*, I promised us both.

A nurse appeared behind me. "She's doing really well, getting stronger every day. Do you want to hold her?"

I couldn't believe my ears. She said I could hold my daughter for the first time since her birth, skin to skin! The nurse opened the incubator and adjusted some of Victoria's tubes and wires. She placed my baby in my arms, and suddenly everything was magical. Victoria looked like an angel with her beautiful brown eyes blinking up at me. I wondered if she knew I was her mother.

My eyes filled with grateful tears. Victoria was a fighter who survived when almost everybody said she had little to no chance. She fought that battle all on her own. She was a warrior, a true miracle. I realized that if she could be strong and fight so hard, then what excuse did I have for not doing the same thing?

I smiled down at my child as the nurse took a picture of us. She didn't realize how she changed my life with her kindness. I could have held my daughter for hours that day, and I couldn't wait until she came home and I had that opportunity.

I'd been dreading it for weeks, but the day finally came when the rent was due. My landlord, a short Indian man who seemed devoid of any sense of humor, showed up first thing in the morning with his hand outstretched. I put the cash I had in his hand and looked at him woefully.

"It's a little less than half," I admitted, "but I promise to have the rest in a few days."

As predicted, this made the landlord angry. He refused to take the money at first, saying he wanted the whole thing at once, but after a few minutes of my sob story he took the cash. He said he would come back in two days for the rest, turned on his heel and walked away without saying goodbye.

How was I going to come up with the money? I didn't get paid until later in the month, and it wouldn't be enough to cover the rest of the rent and keep us going with food and electricity. Praying to win the lottery hadn't worked so far. I was running out of options.

Two days seemed to whiz by, and still I had come up with nothing. I cried real tears when the landlord came back and swore I would get the money somehow. I'd even pay a late fee if he wanted. He left without a word, and my heart sank knowing my pleas fell on deaf ears. I wasn't surprised when an eviction notice was taped to my door one day later. What was I going to do now?

"Move in with me!" Tricia offered excitedly. "You can pay half my rent, which is less than what you were paying before. We would have a total blast!"

I thought about it. I didn't know Tricia that well, but she seemed cool whenever I spent time with her. It wasn't like I was fielding any other offers for a place to stay either. The only problem was that she didn't invite Brandon and Shawn to move in with me. "My house isn't that big," Tricia protested.

My heart simply broke in that moment. The boys would have to stay with Eric for a while until I saved more money. I felt incredible shame for not being able to provide for my own kids and give them a happy and stable home. That was all I ever wanted for them. I couldn't risk them having no place to live. Maybe Eric would be willing to temporarily care for them, at least for a while until I found my own place again and got my life straightened out.

Eric had a new live-in girlfriend named Kathy, whom the boys seemed to like a lot. She seemed nice enough, and so much time had passed that I didn't feel jealous. I'd never give up my place as the boys' mother, but I hoped that she would be the soft touch they needed if Eric was ever rigid or harsh with them. He was an awesome father, but he could be strict. Even though it killed me, I had to admit I was not the best provider for Brandon and Shawn.

I sat the boys down on the couch and kept my tears in check as I delivered the news.

"It's only temporary," I promised them. "We'll see each other all the time. When I get everything straightened out, you can live with me again."

Neither Brandon nor Shawn said much. They just nodded at the same time. I could tell they were hurting, and I felt like the worst mother in the world. There was no way I could live without them for very long. It was only logistics and the current money situation, not a reflection of how much I loved them. I had to believe things would go back to normal someday soon and I'd have Brandon, Shawn and Victoria all under my roof again. Anything else was unthinkable.

Chapter Nineteen

Everything went downhill with Tricia
shortly after I moved in. I missed Brandon
and Shawn so terribly that I ended up
spending a lot of time in my rented bedroom
feeling depressed, crying and sleeping
almost all the time.

Tricia only allowed me to bring a fraction
of my stuff, no furniture or anything that
wouldn't fit in one bedroom. It made me
think about my townhouse full of
knick-knacks and pretty decorations I loved,
which were all sold or given away. I used to
be so proud of my home.

At Tricia's, my pride seemed to have not
survived the trip. She was super strict about
"her" house from the very first day. "You're
just my roommate," she reminded me as she
cleaned up a plate and glass I'd
absentmindedly left on the counter. She
didn't want her house or her life disrupted. I
was nothing if not disruptive.

In a twist that was about to mess up Tricia's life even more, the hospital called to tell me Victoria was ready to come home. Tricia agreed to let me put a crib in my room, but she warned me again that she didn't want to have her life disrupted. The nurses at the hospital trained me to give her four-ounce bottles and make sure she drank them completely.

I worked extra hard on the only goal that was stopping me from taking my baby home. Soon enough, I was an expert at feeding my daughter, impressing both the nurses and her doctor. They told me Micah and I had to take a parenting class at the hospital before they would let Victoria leave. I passed the information on to Micah, who showed up to the class drunk and almost got thrown out for being combative with the teacher.

I still hadn't blocked Micah from sending me email. He was furious about my move to Tricia's house, knowing he was not welcome to see me there. It was a relief that he wouldn't be showing up at my bedroom window or front door unexpectedly anymore. I'm sure Tricia would have called the cops. She hated Micah as much as he hated her, and it was like acid on her tongue whenever she said his name.

Tricia tried to take me out to meet other guys, specifically a guitar player named Jason in a local band she followed. Intrigued, I went with her to one of his shows. Being out of the house was refreshing. Tricia and I giggled over how cute Jason was. She also brought along friends from her job at the post office to join us. They laughed at us acting like schoolgirls even though the guitar player only gave me a lukewarm greeting on introduction.

One of Tricia's friends, Mark, found my behavior particularly amusing and joked that he wished he played the guitar, too. I took a group picture of all of us, and Mark gave me his email address so he could get a copy. I sent the picture as soon as I got back to Tricia's place.

The next morning, it surprised me to see that Mark had written me a long email back. He wrote about what a pleasure it was to meet me, how beautiful I was and how he would love to spend more time with someone as wonderful as me. I tried to remember what I'd done the night before to appear so irresistible and came up empty.

It was difficult to understand how a total stranger could say those things about me without knowing who I was at all. Even so, I was curious enough to suggest to Mark that we hang out as friends and see what happens. He took me to the occasional dinner and the movies and never pressured me for more. I was grateful for the distraction from missing my kids so much and feeling trapped in Tricia's bedroom.

I didn't tell Micah about my new friend. I'm sure he would have called me every name in the book while trashing Mark at the same time. Tricia kept pointing out that Mark had a good stable job as a mailman, a house he owned and a bright future. She wanted me to be free of Micah forever and believed Mark was the solution.

The day finally came when I could take Victoria home. She was still such a tiny and fragile girl, and I worried I'd screw up taking care of her. I wanted to treat her like the miracle she truly was. Tricia wasn't home for an introduction when we arrived, so I took Victoria into my room and laid her down on my bed. I curled up next to her and stared at her sweet face for hours. She was such a blessing, and I was so proud of her. She was a survivor.

I emailed Micah as a courtesy to tell him Victoria was home. He pleaded with me to bring her to the townhouse where he was still squatting. I wasn't sure if he wanted to meet his daughter or get back into my head again. I stalled for a few days, but then I decided he had the right to see her. Standing outside the front door of my old townhouse with Victoria in my arms, I hoped I was making the right decision. From the outside, the home I had once loved so much looked almost dilapidated with garbage strewn about and the hedges overgrown.

Micah met me in the doorway and took Victoria out of my arms. He held her close and whispered in her ear, telling her that Daddy loved her. I walked past them into the living room, which looked a hundred times worse than the day I moved out. The whole house was dark, filthy and depressing. I imagined what it would be like to live in that squalor day after day, not knowing when the police would kick you out. Micah's stress level had to be through the roof. I was glad it wasn't my problem anymore. The townhouse was his now.

I didn't stay there long because it was still hard to look at. The house no longer held any hope, promise or plans for the future. It was impossible to picture watching Brandon or Shawn playing in their room or sitting at the kitchen table with them sharing a meal anymore. Remembering my excitement from the first day when the movers came now made me feel depressed.

Since I worked from home and had a three-month-old baby, I didn't have a lot of options for a social life. Trying to keep Victoria quiet was my biggest job. Tricia was easily irritated, and I was deathly afraid of a confrontation. It wasn't like I didn't warn her ahead of time that a baby was coming. Victoria and my living situation depended on Tricia staying as calm as possible.

"This is MY house, Glenna," she repeated
often, usually amid cleaning up the
occasional glass or baby bottle I left in the
sink. I spent a lot more time isolating myself,
not using the living room or other common
areas we shared. Tricia and I stopped going
out places together. We completely stopped
talking to each other. I felt like a prisoner of
circumstance, trapped in a bedroom with my
infant daughter because of my own bad
decisions.

At Eric's invitation, I picked up the boys
so they could meet Victoria. Since they
weren't welcome at Tricia's, I drove us over
to a park near Eric's house. I laid Victoria
gently across my lap so Brandon and Shawn
could get a good look at her. They couldn't
stop smiling and staring.

"Hello, little Bictoria," Shawn said in his
sweetest voice.

Then the questions started. When could
they live with me again? Why did I have to
stay at my friend's house?

"I don't even care if you live with Micah," Shawn said bravely. "I just want to be with you."

I sat at the bottom of the slide with my baby daughter in my arms with hot tears overflowing my eyes. There was nothing I wanted more than to take Brandon and Shawn home with me right then, but I'd blown it big time. The shame I felt was suffocating. Brandon didn't say much, having four years on Shawn and a better ability to understand. He turned his head away when he saw me crying. *Was I losing him already?*

The next time Mark took me out to dinner, I brought Victoria along in her car seat. Mark fell in love with her instantly, fussing over her and worrying if she needed anything like a bottle, a diaper change or a burp. When he held her in his arms, she never cried. Mark was far more attentive to Victoria than her own father. It was great to see them bonding, and in that moment I wished I loved him.

Not long after that, I developed a cough

out of nowhere that wouldn't go away. It felt like there was mucus in my lungs that wouldn't budge. After a week went by with no improvement, I went to a nearby emergency room. They diagnosed me with pneumonia, gave me a bunch of medications and told me to rest as much as possible. I tried to heed the doctor's advice, but I still had a newborn and rent to pay.

When I pushed myself too hard, my body took over and shut down. I ended up spending two weeks in bed, only getting up to take care of Victoria. I'd never felt so terrible in my life. Even Tricia became concerned and knocked to check on me every so often. When I lied and told her I was fine, she shut the door without another word.

Lying there in bed, I spent a lot of time feeling sorry for myself. Not only was it unproductive, but it made my depression even worse. On the bed next to me was a piece of paper Shawn had given me the last time we were at the park. He told me it was a card. When I unfolded it, he'd written, "I misu" in tiny letters. I couldn't stop reading it even though it hurt every single time. The truth was that I missed my boys desperately, and it felt like they were a million miles away.

Micah continued to send me messages, demanding that I bring over the baby to see him. I guessed from his prior disinterest in Victoria that he was using her as a pawn. The line between sticking to my guns and allowing Victoria to visit with her father was blurry. Micah badgered until he wore me down. His guilt trips got the better of me. I packed up our daughter again and took her back to the townhouse for a visit. Micah held Victoria for about five minutes before starting in on me.

"You could always come back," he cajoled. "You shouldn't have to do this all by yourself. You have nobody to help you, but I would help with everything."

Shaking my head no, I gathered Victoria's things to leave. I should have known better. Micah tried to hug me as I left, but I shrugged him off with his words still echoing in my ears. Of course I didn't want to do everything by myself. I wished Victoria had a real father who cared about both of us. If Micah was suggesting we move back into that hellhole of a townhouse, he would have a long wait.

While I was recovering from the pneumonia, I got a phone call from my former sister-in-law. Cheryl used to be married to Eric's brother, and she checked up on me once in a while after Eric and I divorced because she'd been through something similar. Since she lived all the way in Virginia, we hardly ever saw each other in person. Cheryl asked how I was doing, and I told her about Tricia being so unfriendly and Victoria and I being confined in our little bedroom.

"You should come to Virginia," Cheryl said right away. "We have a whole remodeled basement in our house you can live in while you figure out what to do next."

As tempting as the offer was, I told Cheryl I'd have to think about it. There was definitely an upside. I could save money and put major distance between me and Micah;

however, there were Brandon and Shawn to consider. I felt so far away from them already. I'd have to call Cheryl back and tell her no.

Once my pneumonia was gone and I felt stronger, I picked up Brandon and Shawn to take them out to dinner. When I returned home, Tricia had been in my room, and there was a Post-It Note on my desk.

"Were you with Micah tonight? If so, pack your bags."

I couldn't believe my eyes. What was she talking about? First of all, I wasn't with Micah. Second, why was it any of her business? Was my rented room contingent on whether I stayed away from Micah? Would she leave me homeless if she ever "caught" me with him again? I realized then I was completely under Tricia's control, and the thought terrified me. She had become so unpredictable.

The next thing I did was call Cheryl back and take her up on her offer. She was family, and that was a lot better than living with a dictator. I told her it would only be for a short time because of missing the boys. Maybe going to Virginia would give me the opportunity to save money with no rent to pay. Then I could come back to Florida in a few months and live with all my children again. It was the only thing I wanted. Brandon and Shawn might be sad about me leaving for a little while, but it would end up with a fresh start for all of us. We didn't need any more crazy people coming into our lives and messing up our family. It was time for us to be free.

Chapter Twenty

Cheryl's house in Virginia sat high on a hill and was the size of a mansion. There were three stories in all, and I had the whole basement to myself. It didn't look like any basement I'd ever seen. I felt like I had an upscale apartment, complete with a huge plasma TV and stereo system with a giant pool table in the middle of the living room. There was a bedroom off to the side for Victoria and me to sleep in. Tucked away in the corner of the basement was a wine cellar and a refrigerator full of imported beer. It seemed like the perfect place to bide my time while I saved money to return to Florida.

"When Victoria starts walking, she'll have lots of room inside and outside to run around," Cheryl told me as she held my daughter in her arms.

Soon after we arrived, Cheryl took us to the Washington Zoo and pushed Victoria in a stroller all around the park. All the beauty and history of the city was inspiring, and I wanted Victoria to experience all of it. We could take the subway to the mall every day and never run out of things to do. I enjoyed the cool air after the stifling weather in Florida even though it was spring. It felt like being reborn.

Victoria and I were spoiled by Cheryl's family. She was remarried from Eric's brother to a nice man named Tom. Their four children, who were teenagers, took turns holding and playing with Victoria. My little girl's smiles and giggles warmed my heart. She could finally make as much noise as she wanted.

Cheryl and Tom invited us to every activity their family wanted to do. Cheryl also spent time working with Victoria, helping build up her muscles and encouraging her to stand. I could tell they already loved her, and it made me sad to think of how bummed they would be when Victoria and I went back to Florida.

I set up an office in the basement for transcription and vowed to work every extra hour I could. With no real friends in

Virginia, I wouldn't be distracted from work. I became a hermit, spending almost all my time on the computer while Victoria played with the other kids. I'd grab a beer from the fridge or a glass of wine and keep working until I needed a refill. The tipsier I got, the more time I spent on Facebook posting and chatting rather than getting work done. The alcohol made me feel jittery the next day, and I'd either have to drink some more or stay in bed and not work at all.

Being stuck in the basement made me stir crazy after about a month. I was miserable without the boys and lonely for friends to hang out with. There was nobody I knew in Virginia except Cheryl and her family, and they couldn't be expected to entertain me all the time.

I realized I was still in a prison, just a different type of cage, and I'd put myself there. When I stopped coming upstairs to visit with the family, Cheryl came into my room to ask me what my future plans were. Had I saved any money or looked for a job that paid more? The truth was, I'd done neither of these things. Any little bit of money I brought in seemed to evaporate, mostly at the local mall when I got bored sitting around the house. I continued to make the same mistakes I did in Florida, bringing all my bad habits with me and doing nothing to change them.

Micah emailed me almost every day after I arrived in Virginia. He wanted to know what I was going to do after my time at Cheryl's house and hoped it would include him. He'd finally gotten evicted from the townhouse when the bank had taken it over, and he told me he'd found a new place in West Palm Beach. Micah promised me his feelings hadn't changed. He loved me more than ever and wanted to be a dad to Victoria and work things out.

I'd heard it all before, but the drunk and lonely woman in me still listened. I started looking forward to his emails, and at one point I even told Micah I loved him back. Even though I was drunk when I wrote it, when Micah asked me if I meant it, I said yes. My memories of the past were blurry through a constant lens of alcohol, and I conveniently forgot how horrible some of

them were. Micah made me feel wanted
again, like I was important to somebody. I
was desperate for companionship and
somebody to hold me and adore me. There
was little chance of that happening in
Cheryl's basement.

After a few weeks back and forth, Micah
and I made plans to see each other in person.
I took what little money I had and bought
him a plane ticket to fly to Virginia. When I
described Cheryl's tricked-out house to
Micah, both of us imagined how much fun it
would be if we spent the weekend in the
basement playing pool and watching
movies.

Cheryl was not so naive, however. She
already had an earful of Micah's
transgressions thanks to me, so it would be a
hard sell to get her to let him stay. When I
approached her, she told me she would
think about it and let me know. Two days
went by without a word, but then she asked
me to meet her in the upstairs library.

"I've been thinking about it," Cheryl said
as I sat across from her on the couch. "Micah

can't stay here. We're going out of town this weekend. Some of the kids are staying behind, but I don't want Micah around them. I also have this house to worry about."

I knew Cheryl wasn't a big fan of Micah, but suddenly I felt protective of him. It seemed unfair of her to turn him into a monster. Her kids were nearly grown adults. What damage could Micah do to them? As far as her house, I was sure Micah could handle a day or two without breaking anything or being too loud. It seemed like Cheryl was predicting doom for no reason, but I had to accept her decision as I had no ground to stand on.

When I gave Micah the news over the phone, he started crying and told me how disappointed he was. I promised I would try to scrape enough cash together for a motel room if he came up anyway, but that getting the money would take a while. Micah did not want to wait. He felt we were on the verge of getting back together and didn't want anything to spoil it. Wasn't there something we could do?

An idea formed in my mind. Cheryl said she would be out of town for the weekend. If I was careful, maybe I could sneak Micah through the basement side door. The kids who didn't go on the trip would never know the difference. They never came downstairs to see me anyway. It would only be for a day or two. I'd even admit the truth to Cheryl later on. She had to understand how lonely I was. Besides, wouldn't it be good news to see a marriage put back together and not end in divorce?

I shared my plan with Micah, who was more than willing. He already had the plane ticket I bought him, and it seemed like the perfect solution. I told Cheryl that Micah was still coming to visit but would stay in a nearby hotel. She rolled her eyes as if the entire state of Virginia was not big enough to separate Micah from me or her family.

When I told her Micah and I might reconcile, she left the room without comment. Her attitude confused me. She'd been through a bad divorce, so I expected her to be on the side of keeping a marriage together.

The day finally came when Victoria and I picked up Micah at the airport. I wore something I knew he would like, a black lace top with a brown leather miniskirt and thigh-high boots. As I waited for him in the luggage terminal, I paused for a moment. What was I doing? Did I really want to get back together with someone who treated me and my sons so badly?

None of the few people left in my life were going to be supportive of our relationship, especially not after the character assassination I'd done on him. I kept telling myself that I was one of the few who knew the "real" Micah. Everyone else just misunderstood him. Not everything was always black and white.

Suddenly, I saw Micah walking toward me. I stopped myself from breaking into a run to greet him, not that I could have run in my stiletto boots. Waiting until he got within reach, I stretched my arms out to hug him tight. He seemed distracted and nervous and barely looked like he saw me or Victoria at all.

"Are you sure this will work?" he asked me as I drove him to the motel. We'd scraped up enough to buy him one night's stay, but it left us both without much money.

"Of course," I assured him. "We can spend the day in Washington D.C. tomorrow going to museums and stuff. By that time, Cheryl and her husband will have left for their trip. Then we can go to her house and I can sneak you in the side door."

Micah gave me a troubled look but smiled. He reached down and patted Victoria on her head. Our baby smiled back sweetly at him. "Okay," he said. "Let's do it."

We arrived in the city the next day and took Victoria to the Smithsonian. I took turns with Micah pushing her around in her stroller. We returned to the Washington Zoo, and Micah delighted in all the animals and spent most of his time talking to them. "You're a good giraffe, nice giraffe," he said as Victoria giggled over his excitement.

It made me happy that we were all getting

along so well. Maybe things would work out after all. However, as the day grew later, I felt nervous. What if staying at Cheryl's house was a terrible plan? What if one of the kids busted me? Suddenly, it seemed like the worst idea I'd ever had. I tried to keep up a brave front for Micah, but I was losing my nerve. Micah had no money and no other place to go. I couldn't just leave him out on the street.

The sky was dark when we drove up near Cheryl's house. There were lights on upstairs like somebody was home. I parked the car on the side of the driveway and told Micah to wait outside with Victoria, tiptoeing up the walkway only to discover Tom waiting for me at the front entrance.

"WHAT ARE YOU DOING?" he yelled at me. I'd never seen him so furious before. My whole body trembled as I tried to form words. No excuse was coming to me, and I knew I had to talk fast.

"I… I don't know," I sputtered. "I'll be back in a little while."

I ran back down the driveway and headed straight for the car where Micah and Victoria were waiting.

"Cheryl wants to talk to you," Tom shouted after me as I hurried away.

I jumped in the driver's seat with my heart pounding, feeling the first signs of a panic attack. I'd never been so terrified in my life. When I told Micah what happened, he kept repeating "oh shit" over and over as we drove away. I was crying so hard that it woke up Victoria in her car seat. All I wanted to do was get as far away from Cheryl's house as possible. What the hell was I thinking?

"Why don't we get another motel?" Micah suggested. I checked my bank account balance from my cell phone, already certain it was almost empty. There wasn't enough money for one night anywhere, and Micah didn't have a cent to his name. He'd spent what little he had to make the trip to Virginia. Not knowing where else to go, I drove us to Walmart where we pushed Victoria around the store in her stroller. It was getting late, and I wished she were asleep in her little crib instead of caught up in this mess I'd created. As I walked aimlessly up and down the aisles, my mind raced a hundred miles an hour. It was impossible to talk or think straight. Micah walked along next to me in silence. This was bad... really bad!

"Call Cheryl," Micah finally said. I knew he was right, but it would take every ounce of bravery I had. Victoria and I had no home anymore and no place to go. I'd have to face whatever Cheryl threw at me. If I didn't, my daughter and I would have to spend the night in my car.

"Cheryl, I'm so sorry," I said as soon as she picked up.

"I want you out of here," Cheryl shouted. "You have betrayed me in the worst way after everything I've done for you! You've already lost your boys, and you'll lose your little girl if you don't change your ways."

I didn't try to defend myself. There was nothing else I could say except that I would come back to get our stuff in the morning. I'd screwed up beyond belief, and to Cheryl I was a lost cause. In my heart, I knew she was right. I was selfish and impulsive, and now it was time to pay the price. My free ride was over. Micah could always fly back home, but Victoria and I were essentially homeless.

In desperation, Micah called his mother for enough money to stay in a motel for one night and drive back to Florida. I was grateful that he didn't abandon me and use his ticket to fly home to Florida by himself.

After we checked into our motel room, I sat on the bed numb and still in shock. One day earlier, I had an amazing place to stay and an extended family who loved me; now I had neither. What would people say when I showed up back in town unexpectedly? There would be a lot of explaining and apologizing to do.

Micah sat down on the bed and put his arm around my waist.

"Don't worry," he said. "I'm going to take care of you and Victoria. Everything will be great. You'll see."

I had no choice but to believe him.

Chapter Twenty-One

I drove my car all the way from Virginia to Florida with Micah in the passenger's seat. He didn't have a valid license, but he seemed to have no problem telling me what a bad driver I was.

"Faster,...slower,...get in the other lane!"

He yelled throughout the entire trip. I followed his orders, not caring which lane I was in. It scared me to think of the hell I would face when we finally arrived back in Palm Beach County. How was I going to explain to the boys that I was with Micah again? How could I explain that to anybody? I'd thrown away what little progress I'd made for a foolish, irresponsible weekend. Impulsive was the kindest word people would use, although stupid applied nicely.

Micah gave me directions once we got to West Palm Beach. I was grateful for a place to hibernate until I figured out what to do next. It was too early to see or talk to anybody yet. There was no way I could spin the story and make it look any better. The bottom line was that I'd screwed up.

We pulled up to a house nearly hidden by overgrown brush, settled in the middle of one of the worst neighborhoods in the city. Out front were a few people sitting in patio chairs smoking cigarettes. Micah waved hello to them.

"Are they your neighbors?" I asked Micah.

"No," he replied. "They live here too."

I followed Micah to the back of the house and through the door that led to his room. There was a filthy mattress on the floor and not much else. Dirt and grime covered the tiles. There was a little TV on top of a stained wooden dresser that was falling apart. I put down my suitcase and sat down cross-legged on the floor. My plan was to sleep for a week straight. Poor Victoria looked exhausted like she needed sleep as much as I did. Suddenly, I heard noises coming from outside the bedroom.

"Do you have roommates?" I asked Micah.

"Yeah, about five or six. They're okay, but sometimes they steal your food. You should keep your stuff in our room."

The bedroom door opened then, and an older man with gray hair stood in front of us. He talked to Micah and ignored me as if I weren't sitting right next to him. I wondered how casually people in the house walked into other people's rooms and whether that was going to be a problem.

I had milk for Victoria, so I went in search of the kitchen to put it in the fridge hoping nobody would steal it from her. We were already low on the money Micah's mother gave us. I wasn't sure how many more cartons of milk it would buy. Victoria needed diapers as well, so we'd have to set aside money for that.

The kitchen matched the rest of the house. I tried not to notice the ants and the occasional roach that scuttled by. The whole main part of the house was blistering hot. Micah told me that the landlord wouldn't let them use the central air conditioning. He had a fan that kept us comfortable, but I wondered what kind of landlord would want a bunch of sweaty, hot and agitated people leaving the house a wreck?

I settled Victoria down in her portable crib and stroked her head until she went to sleep. She went through the whole ordeal right along with us. I wondered if she was old enough to miss Cheryl and her family. They loved her so much and doted on her the whole time we were in Virginia.

I felt ashamed of the way I'd taken so many people out of Victoria's life in such a short time, especially her older brothers. My eyes burned from too much crying, but I shook my tears away. This was no time to be hysterical. I had to come up with a plan to first move us out of this nasty house and then try to repair as much damage as I could.

Micah and I were increasingly on each other's nerves due to the heat and depressing conditions. He seemed a lot more interested in hanging out smoking with his roommates than paying attention to his wife and daughter. I couldn't even work to pass the time because there was no Internet connection. I called my boss and told her I was working on getting back online as soon as possible. There was no way I could lose my job on top of everything else. It was the only thread I was hanging by.

I looked forward to my next paycheck showing up in my bank account so we could escape this hellhole. Even if we had to stay at a motel, it would be preferable to our current situation.

I still hadn't spoken to anyone to let them know I was back in town. Some of my family and a few friends called and left me messages, worried about where I'd gone after leaving Virginia. I guessed word was out about my huge mistake. Even if I wanted to talk, I had no privacy at the house. Micah and I stayed cooped up in the bedroom most of the time. There were people coming and going everywhere.

Finally, I called Eric while Micah was at the store. I had to know how the boys were doing.

"What happened?" Eric's voice was slightly anxious. "Cheryl said you packed up and left."

"She threw me out," I cried in a bid for sympathy. "Just like that, she left me on the street."

"Did you try to sneak Micah into her house?" When Eric said it out loud, it sounded a thousand times worse.

"Could you please let the boys know I'll see them as soon as I can?"

Eric agreed and we hung up. There wasn't much left for either of us to say. I could tell how disappointed he was in me. No way could I ask for his help, not again.

Micah and I started apartment shopping as soon as my next paycheck arrived. I didn't have enough for first, last and security, so we looked for something we could pay by the week. There were a few places in Lake Worth, not the nicest city in South Florida, but my demands were simple. Some privacy and a clean place to stay were all we needed. Micah still had his landscaping job, so I hoped between the two of us we could stay up to date with rent and other expenses.

We moved immediately the day we found a one-room studio. The neighborhood was only slightly better, but there were no roommates to deal with. There wasn't much stuff to move. All of it fit in the backseat of my car. I had clothes, makeup, a few books and two large Tupperware bins filled with my children's pictures and artwork. There was also my little black rocking chair that my grandfather gave me when I was five. I couldn't part with it. It was a link to happier times, and I hoped to give it to Victoria when she was old enough to sit in it.

The next few days came with a sense of relief. The studio had Internet access bundled into the rent, so I got back to work the day after we moved. I tried to make the best of a bad situation. Sometimes I thought about my townhouse and pictured the boys chasing each other up and down the stairs and playing video games in the living room. I wished I could still tuck them in at night and ask them about their favorite thing that happened each day.

When I thought about things like that, I had to push the memories aside before I let them drive me crazy. If I allowed depression to swallow me up again, I feared I would never come out of it. Alcohol remained my emotional painkiller even though it always failed me by the next morning, leaving me anxious and shaky. It was hard to let Micah go to work every day. I was frightened of being left alone with my thoughts.

Micah and I still fought often. Harsh words replaced the kind words he'd spoken to me in Virginia. Whenever I got emotional about Brandon and Shawn, he became angry and combative.

"Those are Eric's boys now," he insisted. "It's too late for anything else. You've already blown it. Why don't you focus on OUR daughter?"

I hated him for saying it because it was true. Micah called me unstable and selfish. He said I was lucky to have him taking care of me because nobody else would have me. Every one of his words stung deep. Why had I let him back into my life? I never said that out loud, not wanting to be mean like him. He was also the only person standing between me and homelessness.

There was also the fact that he was Victoria's father. I mistakenly thought I owed my little girl an intact family after everything I'd put her through. She was the sweetest and most quiet baby in the world. She hardly ever cried, even when Micah and I were fighting. My poor baby acted like she didn't want to be too much trouble. She deserved so much better. I whispered promises I couldn't keep to Victoria in her little crib and told her that everything would work out fine. She looked up at me and smiled, too young to realize I wasn't confident in my words.

Micah made "friends" in our new neighborhood who kept him out of the apartment more often. I had no interest in meeting any of the neighbors. I'd already seen them out front shouting, drinking and fighting one too many times. I thought it was better to keep to myself. Maybe I should have paid more attention to those people. Even if I never walked out my front door, that didn't mean terrible things couldn't come inside. Evil is tricky like that.

Chapter Twenty-Two

"Glenna, hey, wake up!"

I opened my eyes into darkness, barely
able to see Micah shaking me awake. My
heart instantly pounded at the thought that
something was wrong. I remembered Micah
had left the apartment earlier in the evening.
Did something bad happen?

"Here," Micah said as he stretched his arm
toward me. "Take this."

He opened his hand to reveal a tiny blue
pill almost the size of a crumb. He smiled
proudly as he put it in my hand.

"What is it?" I asked, now fully awake.
"It's the middle of the night."

"Put it in your mouth, under your tongue.
I'll get you some water."

I dutifully placed the pill under my tongue
while Micah went to the kitchen. He may

have been capable of a lot of things, but I didn't think he was trying to poison me. The thought of being high for a few hours instead of miserable was most welcome. I swallowed the pill with the water Micah brought me. Victoria slept soundly in her crib, and when I glanced her way I felt a twinge of guilt. It was too late to turn back, but I prayed I'd be okay before morning when she woke up.

The pill hit me about 15 minutes later while I was still lying in bed. I felt a sudden overall warmth followed by massive tingling throughout my body. It felt like I was all lit up, and I got out of bed to greet the amazing sensations I was having.

For the first time in ages, nothing in the world seemed wrong. My constant anxiety was gone, and I felt like nothing bad could touch me. I gave Micah a surprised look, but he only smiled at me. His eyes seemed glazed over, and I quickly figured out he had taken the same kind of pill.

"What was that?" I asked him. I'd never felt so amazing in my entire life.

"A Roxy," Micah answered.

I didn't really care what its name was. It was a miracle, and I never wanted the effects to stop. How could I go back to my usual chaotic and depressed state after experiencing nirvana?

"Where did you get it?" I asked.

Micah shrugged, "From the chick who lives behind us. She's sort of a pimp, and she also sells pills."

It didn't occur to me to ask why Micah was hanging out with a drug-dealing pimp because as of now she was my new best friend. I felt like I was alive for the first time in ages, ready to take on the entire world.

Micah and I spent the rest of the night watching movies, playing 80s music and dancing around our tiny apartment quietly so we didn't wake up Victoria. Micah seemed glad to see his normally anxious wife gone, with a loving and happy woman in her place.

We finally went to sleep right before the sun came up. I knew Victoria would be up soon and need me. When I heard her cry a few hours later, I stumbled to the kitchen for a bottle. The Roxy had completely worn off, leaving me with a sad and void feeling inside. I mourned the loss of feeling happy and carefree.

Micah heard Victoria and sat up in bed. He'd gotten much less sleep than I had, and his cranky attitude showed it. I ignored his comments about the baby making too much noise. There was only one question I wanted to ask him.

"When can we get more?"

Chapter Twenty-Three

Time became divided by being high and waiting to get high. The little blue pills, when we could get them, became our entire lives. When I had one, I didn't feel pain or depression or anything else. Micah and I bought a box of straws so we could snort them instead of swallowing them. We got high a lot more quickly that way. The pimp girl behind us still sold us our fix, but sometimes she was out of the Roxy pills and we had to improvise with something else. Luckily, there was no shortage of people in our neighborhood who either sold them or knew someone who did.

From the first time the opiate entered my body, I saw a new way to live and embraced it. I didn't have to worry about the things I'd done or people I'd lost. For those few short hours the pill lasted, I was at total peace. I wished the feeling would last forever. When Micah and I couldn't get the drugs, we both suffered from physical and emotional pain from opiate withdrawal. My depression and anxiety became extreme when I felt anything besides high. I'd sob for my lost children, for myself, for the bad hand life had dealt me. My sadness was magnified without the pills, and I swore I'd find some way to never be without them again.

Being a drug addict turned out to be a full-time job. Waiting was always the hardest part. Our dealer would make a promise to deliver, but we sometimes had to wait hours or days. During that time, I wasn't able to work or clean the apartment or see anybody. Micah would go to his landscaping job and come home to find me curled up in bed in tears, having spent the entire day in that position.

During the most desperate hours, I'd drive myself to the emergency room with a ready-made excuse to get a shot of morphine. I guess I didn't look like a typical addict yet, so the ER doctors always provided me with what I needed. The effect was always temporary though, and I'd be stuck in withdrawal again a few hours later.

I asked for money from the few friends

who would still talk to me. It wasn't a huge amount, twenty or forty dollars at a time, but it was enough to buy a few pills to hold me over. In the beginning I shared my stash with Micah, but as my addiction grew stronger I made a habit of hiding it from him whenever I had drugs. I wasn't willing anymore to give up half of what I had to him or anyone else.

If I had a Roxy, I could do my transcription work and clean the apartment. I didn't have to feel anything, no pain from loss or aching in my heart. When the drug wore off, I felt ashamed about what I was doing to my life. The agony of losing my boys was unbearable, and I wasn't doing right by Victoria even though she wasn't aware of what was happening. *Congratulations,* I told myself. *You're nothing but a junkie now.*

I didn't care that what I was doing was dangerous. Micah and I were associating with the shadiest people in the city to get our drugs. They were dealers and users, and some of them regularly spent time in jail. They had needle tracks on their arms and missing teeth, and they scared the hell out of me. It didn't matter, though, as long as they had what I wanted. I promised myself I'd never end up like them, not sure if I believed it.

I only saw my boys once every couple of months. I couldn't do it unless I took a pill first. My guilt was too much to bear, and I was afraid I'd cry the entire time. Eric no longer let me in his house since I was still with Micah doing "God knows what." I met Brandon and Shawn at the park near their house or at the closest McDonald's. Most of the time, I didn't have much to say to either of them. They didn't need to hear about how much I hated myself and how disgusting I felt.

It was impossible to parent my children for an hour every couple of months. I listened to them tell me about school and their friends. They played with Victoria, whom they missed as much as me. They knew they couldn't come to my apartment because of Micah, but they begged to come anyway. All they wanted was to be with their mother.

My heart broke over and over during our visits, and after a while I found excuses not to have them anymore. They were better off without me. Eric's girlfriend, Kathy, seemed like she was motherly. I was grateful to her for cuddling them, feeding them and tucking them into bed, even as I wished I were doing those things.

The arguments between me and Micah progressed. They were always either drug fueled or because of a lack of drugs. Micah berated me whenever he wasn't getting his way, calling me a disgusting drug addict and a horrible parent. I burst into tears regularly as he pushed every single button I had. He knew exactly how to hurt me and never held back. He stole money from my purse and would sneak away for hours. I was more furious at the thought that he was using drugs without me than I was about the money.

The fights became physical with Micah. He once pushed me into our kitchen table. He grabbed me by the arms and shook me hard to get me to listen to him. He trapped me in our bathroom and pinned me down on the bed and yelled at me. I tried to fight back, but he was much stronger. There was nothing I could do but complain about how bad he was treating me. I conveniently left out the part about using drugs myself. Playing the victim usually worked until people got tired of trying to help me and could no longer watch as I tore my life apart.

If I ever forgot how evil and selfish I was, I had Micah there to remind me. He said I used and manipulated people to get what I wanted. Micah told me I was empty inside and didn't have a soul. I knew he was right. It had to be true. I felt nothing inside when I was high. It became hard to get the same high after a while. My tolerance to narcotics built up so much that I was horribly sick without them and instead wished for death.

Micah kept telling me that my boys belonged to Eric and that I should focus on Victoria and him. That was the problem, though. I couldn't focus at all. My little girl was healthy and growing, and I should have been grateful every day for it. Instead, I treated her as an afterthought. I knew it was only a matter of time before all the skeletons poured out of my closet and I lost her, too. Everything in life was so temporary. I couldn't count on anything or anybody except Micah. Without him taking care of me, I couldn't function.

One day, Micah told me he was having terrible pain in his hips and needed to go to the emergency room. I rolled my eyes, thinking he was faking it to get pills like I'd done. When we checked in at the hospital, the doctor took x-rays that showed both of Micah's hips totally degenerated from avascular necrosis. He would need hip replacements on both sides. Micah tried to seem upset when he said, "I guess I need to see a pain doctor now," but I was sure he was thrilled about it.

I felt jealous at all the pills he would get. He had to have surgery, but he set up the visit at the pain clinic first. His new doctor wrote him a prescription for 90 oxycodone at 30 milligram strength. When he came home, he showed me the bottle and said he would share as long as I didn't get too greedy. I asked him for one on the spot, and within minutes I was feeling on top of the world.

I never knew how many pills Micah was taking in one day, but they didn't seem to make him happy anymore. He nodded off in front of the TV and stumbled around the apartment knocking things over. The thought of never running out of drugs again was comforting, but at least I knew when to watch my dose. I didn't want to become a zombie like Micah. He scared me when he was like that. He was drinking on top of the drugs, and I was afraid he would overdose right on the couch. What was I supposed to do then?

During one weekend, Micah and I stayed up late listening to music and partying with drugs and alcohol. Micah said he was feeling generous and kept handing out extra pills from his prescription bottle. I felt great until I suddenly didn't. My body became heavy and my words were slurred. I wanted to lie down in bed and just go to sleep for a long time.

"Glenna, wake up!"

Micah was standing over me, lightly slapping my face.

"Leave me alone," I mumbled. "Wanna sleep."

"Get up right now!" Micah pulled me out of bed by the arm. "You're overdosing and you can't go to sleep!"

"Go away," I told him. "Leave me alone."

Micah put his arm around me and led me outside. He put Victoria in her stroller and pushed it while he dragged me around the neighborhood. My legs didn't seem to be working, and I couldn't keep up with Micah's fast pace. Shadowy faces of neighbors came in and out of focus as I staggered up and down the streets. I felt so dizzy and sick.

The next morning, I was furious at Micah for trying to save me. Why didn't he leave me alone and let me go to sleep and never wake up? There would have been no more pain, no more being hungry from lack of food, no more crying for all I'd lost. He kept asking me to thank him for saving my life, but instead I told him I'd never forgive him. I'd gotten so close to being put out of my misery. Surely nobody would miss me, not even my kids. I was no good for them anyway. Having a mother like me would only hurt them in the long run.

I didn't talk to Micah for the rest of that day, believing that his rescue only prolonged my suffering. Our life as addicts was terrible, but living together was becoming hell.

Chapter Twenty-Four

In the days of active addiction when I felt well enough to pick up the boys, I always waited at the end of the driveway for them to come out of their house. I never wanted to see Eric or the look of pity on his face. He would have asked questions. He always had questions. Unfortunately, I had no good answers.

I knew I looked like shit and felt even worse. It scared me that he might notice the change in me and not let me see the boys anymore. My relationship with Brandon and Shawn was hanging by a thread as it was. "They're Eric's boys," Micah repeated. "There's nothing you can do to change that."

It felt like he was telling the truth. I struggled to think of things to talk about with Brandon and Shawn. I didn't share anything about my life with them. All I cared about was if they were happy and enjoying their days, but I didn't know how to ask them anything without dissolving into tears.

Remembering them as the little boys who adored me was too much to bear. Ever since they were born, I had so many things I wanted to teach them. Now I didn't feel like I had the right to try. The knowledge tore my heart into shreds. Thinking of either one of my sons needing me for something could send me to bed for an entire day. The pills helped me forget, but the pain always came back.

One Saturday afternoon at pickup, Eric followed the boys to the end of the driveway. I took a deep breath and opened my car door. Gathering the boys into a big hug, I focused every ounce of my attention on them. If I didn't make eye contact with Eric, maybe he wouldn't want to talk. I didn't want to see the look of disappointment in his face. The boys scrambled happily into my back seat, but Eric didn't turn and walk back to the house.

"How is everything?" he finally asked.

"It's fine. Why?"

"We don't hear from you much anymore,"

Eric said. "I just wanted to see if everything was okay."

In that moment, I wanted to tell him the truth. I was miserable. I was on drugs. I couldn't put a whole day together without a breakdown. Instead, I nodded my head and assured Eric that everything was fine. I made it sound as believable as possible, but the look in his eyes said he wasn't buying it.

I took Brandon and Shawn to the park and apologized for my absence the way I always did. Neither boy looked up from digging in the dirt and just nodded their heads. I felt like the worst parent alive. My heart ached for the simple things we used to do like cuddling in front of the TV and making silly jokes. I wished I'd appreciated what a gift that was. They told me all their secrets then, and I kept them safely locked in my heart. Brandon came and sat next to me, but he didn't say a word. He looked so stoic, already building walls to keep from hurting.

After I dropped the boys off at home, I drove away thinking of Brandon's face at the park. It seemed like he went blank. Would I never see a genuine laugh or heartfelt cry from him again? Would he save all that for Eric and his girlfriend? Even if I had a mountain of pills, would it ever be enough to stop the pain in my heart? When I got back to the apartment, I felt a sense of urgency as I went to turn on my computer. Micah was out somewhere, and I was grateful for it. He wouldn't have let me cry over the boys in the first place much less reach out to anyone else.

"I need help." I typed in Facebook Messenger. Then I hit send as quickly as I could before I lost my nerve.

Eric responded within one minute, "What's going on?"

I told him everything. Micah and I were addicted to narcotics. Micah was an abusive jerk. I almost died of an overdose. Sparing no details, I typed as fast as I could to get everything out.

"What can I do to help?" Eric wrote back.

"I don't know what to do," I answered.

"How do I get out of this?"

"Well," Eric reasoned, "you've tried to get away from Micah before, but he always seems to find you. Then you let him manipulate you. Maybe you should think about permanently moving to a different city where it will be harder for him to bother you in person. That way, you'd have a fighting chance."

"I... I'm scared to detox," I admitted. "Every time I don't have pills, I get severely sick and depressed."

"Wouldn't it be worth it to get that stuff out of your system? Tell yourself it's only one more withdrawal and you'll never have to go through it again."

I thought about what Eric said. Maybe I could get a fresh start in a brand new place. I'd have to leave the boys, but once I did better, they could visit me for long weekends and during the summers. As it stood now, even when I was right under their noses, I was a million miles away.

Micah was another story. There had to be no more leaving my email account open to make sure he was okay. I couldn't give him my new number when I changed it. I'd have to block him on Facebook so I couldn't see what he was doing.

For the first time, I realized I'd become as addicted to Micah as I was to the drugs. Every day, I depended on him for every action, every thought. He saw my mind at its weakest and filled it up with nonsense. Now I would have a chance to do things on my own. The thought was exciting yet terrifying.

"I could go to the other coast of Florida to Cape Coral," I suggested in my next message to Eric. It seemed like a good solution. My friends from high school, Tim and Nancy, lived in that city, so Victoria and I wouldn't be all alone there. Micah didn't have a car and couldn't track me down, so I'd be safe from his manipulation.

Eric offered one more time to help me with money to pay for a new apartment. I called Tim and Nancy, and they agreed to look for a place for me and Victoria to live. Once again, I promised everyone I wouldn't let them down and go back to Micah. I was finished with his abuse. He could rot in hell for all I cared.

It was morning when Micah left for work and I threw everything Victoria and I owned into the back of my car. My daughter and I headed west to our new home in Cape Coral. I vowed never to look back.

Chapter Twenty-Five

Tim and Nancy had found a duplex for me near the intercoastal waterway, and I fell in love with it on first sight. My side was bright and airy with over-sized bedrooms and a gorgeous open kitchen. I gave Victoria the master bedroom and took the smaller bedroom for myself. With the rooms partially furnished already, there wasn't much I needed to add. I couldn't take anything that wouldn't fit in my small car, not that I had much to begin with.

My new landlord was a dream. She'd left the apartment spotless and added lots of loving touches. She even folded the toilet paper in the bathrooms into a cute triangle. I was touched that she cared about me and Victoria even though we still hadn't met in person. My new city was turning out to be great.

Our first morning there, I watched the boats passing by in the gulf from my front patio while Victoria scribbled on the sidewalk with chalk. She was ready to start preschool as soon as I could get her enrolled. I was excited about all the new things she would learn and the friends she would make. Gratitude filled my heart all the way around, especially for the people who helped me in my desperation to get away from drugs and from Micah.

I tried to relax for the next couple of days as I went through withdrawal from opiates. It wasn't as bad as I'd envisioned, and I wondered if my newfound happiness overshadowed any physical discomfort I felt.

I still had periods of sharp anxiety and a nervous stomach, but it was so much better than being a slave to those little blue pills. I tried to take care of myself, making sure I slept and ate well. Once I'd gotten through the worst of it, I felt the first stirrings of pride for what I had accomplished in such a short time.

A couple of weeks passed, and I didn't communicate with Micah at all. I wondered if he was trying to find me or if he'd given up on our marriage the way I had. Getting away from him was the most important thing, and I tried to remember that when loneliness set in. For the first time, I'd chosen to live and not just exist.

My landlord didn't allow me to smoke cigarettes in the apartment, and I didn't want to expose Victoria to my smoking, so I set up a lawn chair on the side of the house and smoked outside instead. Sometimes I waved hello to an older man who lived across the yard. He seemed to be friendly, so I didn't mind when he came over to talk as I sat there puffing on my cigarette.

The guy was full of questions. Where was I from? What did I do for work? Who and where was Victoria's father? It turned into a regular thing. I'd sit in my plastic chair, and he would suddenly appear and walk over to visit me. It was almost amusing how he seemed to come out of his place at the same time I went outside, and I wondered if he was watching for me out his window? I felt sorry for him. He seemed lonely and in need of conversation.

The ladies that ran Victoria's new school seemed excited about her starting there. Tears ran down my little girl's eyes on the first day I dropped her off. Victoria and I hadn't spent time apart since her birth. I was glad to see her teacher take her into her arms and try to distract her as I left the building. Victoria was going to love school and learning new things.

When I got home, I called Brandon and Shawn and invited them to come to Cape Coral for the weekend. I planned to drive over and pick them up. Unfortunately, that meant returning to the other side of Florida where Micah still lived, but I told myself I could handle it. I'd make a quick trip to Jupiter and back and I wouldn't even have to see him.

Tim and Nancy were wonderful friends. Victoria and I had a standing invitation to have dinner at their house once a week. It felt like having a family, and we loved every minute. Things were going so smoothly. I worked hard at my job, meeting deadlines and even typing extra hours to make sure we had enough money.

Victoria was happy at her new school and

overjoyed when the boys finally came to visit. Sometimes I felt twinges of loneliness, but the peace and happiness I'd found made up for it in a hundred ways. My anxiety and stress levels reduced to almost being nonexistent. I felt grateful to be finally free of those terrible pills that almost killed me and free of Micah. Things were truly getting better, and I appreciated every single moment of it.

Everything changed the morning I woke up with a splitting migraine. I got them about once a month, but the pain from this one was worse than usual. Trying something as simple as turning my head felt like an icepick in my skull. The Excedrin I took didn't help at all.

It reminded me of the days when even the slightest twinge of pain sent me rushing to the emergency room in hopes I'd get a shot of morphine. It seemed dangerous to entertain that idea now, but I couldn't stop thinking about it. There was no way I could go. I had to pick up Victoria from school soon, and a normal hospital trip could be two to three hours long. The right side of my temple throbbed, and I felt a sick feeling in my stomach. It was definitely a migraine, but there was nothing I could do about it.

I went outside to my smoking chair, lit a cigarette and tried to relax. The Florida sun was blinding me and making the headache worse. It surprised me that my "friend" from across the lawn hadn't come outside, although it was a relief because he'd become creepy in the last few days. One day, he told me I needed a man, and he looked for any excuse to touch my shoulder or try to hug me.

Despite that, I still felt tempted to knock on his door and ask him if he had anything stronger than Excedrin for my headache. Since he was older, maybe he had issues with pain of his own. *Just this one time*, I promised myself. *After that I'll stay away. This pain is so intense I can't stand it.*

Nobody answered the door when I knocked. I looked around at the other houses near me and wondered about the people inside. Could I really go knock on someone's door and ask for a pain pill? Not only was it rude, it was borderline dangerous and definitely illegal, but I was desperate for relief. The neighborhood was calm and quiet with nobody outside but me. How would I even pick the right door to knock on?

At that exact moment, the older lady who lived behind me came outside to hang laundry on her clothesline. She looked to be in her sixties, as best I could tell from far away. I thought about making myself cry before I approached her, but I couldn't conjure up any tears. My bold behavior shocked me. It wasn't the kind of person I was at all, except when I was using drugs. Did I really want to be that person again? Could I really stick to "just once"?

I hurried to cross the lawn before the lady went back inside. Up close, she had tired eyes with an angry look on her face. She eyed me suspiciously as I walked up to her and said hello.

"I'm so sorry to bother you," I said sweetly. "I have a terrible migraine. It's the worst headache I've had in my entire life. I'm really suffering, and I wanted to ask if you might have something I could take for pain?"

The woman considered me for a moment and then spoke. "All I have is half a Roxy."

I stood there flabbergasted by what I'd just heard. I'd walked up to a complete stranger and asked for drugs, and she happened to have my drug of choice. I couldn't tell if it was a blessing or a warning. The woman walked inside to get me half a pill, and I stood there in her yard trying to think fast. Should I even take it from her? What if I relapsed? I didn't realize that my whole train of thought was already a relapse.

My head hurt so bad, and I knew the Roxy would take the pain away in a matter of minutes. How could I turn that down? When the lady came back outside, I gave her a look of concern.

"Are you sure about this?" I asked meekly.

"Yeah, go ahead," the woman said. "My son is getting me more tomorrow."

I thanked her and took the pill and crossed back to my side of the yard, already wondering how the woman's son was planning to provide more drugs for her.

When I got home, I set the half pill down on my kitchen counter. *Nobody will ever have to know*, I decided. *It's just one time, and I won't do it ever again*. I made the pledge even as I knew I was lying. After chewing up the pill to make it work faster, there was no trace of my migraine within a few minutes. I felt euphoric and wonderful again, but my good feelings were mixed with horrible shame at what I'd done.

I already knew I would ask my neighbor for more drugs even before the first pill wore off. Why did I have to be so impulsive and reckless? It always screwed everything up, and here I was in trouble again. I didn't stop to worry about how Victoria and I would eat or if I had enough money to pay rent. Instead, I started mentally counting how many more pills I could buy from the woman with the money I had.

When I walked back over to her house, I realized I didn't even know her name. I never thought to ask. She sent her son outside to talk to me about the pills. He looked to be in his thirties and like he spent a lot of time getting high and languishing on his mother's couch. None of that mattered to me. He was a means to an end, and I didn't care what his name was either.

The son told me that if I wanted more drugs, I would have to give him a ride to get them. I agreed and handed him one hundred dollars. He added that I would have to give him one of the pills as a "service fee." The more he talked, the more it sounded like a bad deal, but it was too late to turn back.

The next morning, after dropping off Victoria at school, the mother and son neighbors piled into my car. It took me a minute to realize we weren't going to a doctor's office as he guided me back into the neighborhood, finally making me stop at a house where he wanted to get out.

"Wait for me on the next street," he said as he jumped out of the car. His mother and I waited as instructed. I was on the verge of having a major panic attack. *What if a cop saw us parked here on the street for no reason? What if I got pulled over with narcotics in my car?* They were questions I should have considered ahead of time, but I was much too far gone to see reason. After about fifteen agonizing minutes, the son finally showed back up with pills in hand. He passed them out, one for him, one for his mother and three for me at twenty dollars a pop.

I looked down at the tiny blue tablets in my hand and marveled at their power. Micah once told me a story about a guy he worked with who sold his Ford truck for a handful of oxycodone. It sounded so stupid at the time, but now I related more than I wanted to admit. I was enslaved once again, risking my home and freedom and Victoria for a quick fix. When we got back to their house, I idled in the driveway so the neighbors could get out of my car, the sooner the better. The son turned to face me instead.

"Have you ever railed a pill before?" he asked me.

"What's that?"

"You know, do it the intravenous way?"

I'd never even considered such a thing. That kind of stuff was for junkies. I was just fine taking the pills by mouth, and I told him so.

"Oh no, it's awesome," he encouraged me. "You'll be higher than ever before in your life."

My curiosity got the better of me, and I followed him through the house and into his bedroom. He told me to hand him one of my pills and then excused himself and came back with a needle wrapped in plastic and a spoon filled with liquid. Then he reached for my arm.

"Wow, you have great veins," he told me.

I'd never considered my veins before as being good or bad, so I looked down at my arm to check them myself. Before I could say anything in response, the guy quickly slipped the needle under my skin.

"I thought we would count to three," I protested as the drug entered my body. He laughed at me, and I felt like the lowest human being alive. Micah said he'd tried needles once or twice in his life, but I'd always been too scared. It also seemed like a degrading thing to do.

When we were done, I left the son's room without speaking, feeling the warmth of the opiate throughout my body. The son pointed at me and laughed because he noticed I was walking on my tiptoes.

"Oh yeah," he said. "You definitely got high."

Somehow I made it back to the duplex. My body felt lit up like a Christmas tree. Checking the time, I had about fifteen minutes left before I had to start transcribing for work. I put the remaining two pills high up on my kitchen windowsill where only I could reach them.

Sitting down at the computer, I nodded in and out while typing my first report. What the son said was true. I'd never been so high in my life. The report sat open on my screen as I drifted in and out of consciousness. *Please wear off by the time I have to pick up Victoria from school*, I begged as if the drugs were something I could control.

After a while, I walked away from the desk and lay down on my couch. Anxiety crept up on me as the hours passed, and my eyes sprang open every time I tried to doze off. My boss logged me off the system because I left the report hanging. I knew I would likely be in serious trouble if I didn't sign back on right away, but there was no way I could focus and give each report the careful consideration it needed. These were people's medical reports, for God's sake. What was I doing?

The pill finally wore off about half an hour before I picked up Victoria. I couldn't even look the preschool staff in the face as I gathered my daughter and her things. My guilt was overwhelming, and I hoped it didn't show. Once I got Victoria settled in back at home, I tried to make up the work I'd missed, but I spent the whole time trying to fend off another panic attack. I'd been the designated driver for a drug deal and then shot the drugs into my arm like a junkie. It felt way worse than anything that happened back in Jupiter.

As the evening grew later, I got a call from my boss. I tried to make up a story about being sick, but unfortunately she wasn't buying it. She fired me over the phone. I couldn't blame her. I'd done this to myself. My stomach rumbled with nervousness, but I felt a great sadness at the same time. What was I going to do now?

There was a knock at my back door. It was the son who stuck the needle in my arm whose name I never asked.

"I wanted to make sure you were okay," he said. "Hey, do you have an extra cigarette?"

I left him at the door and went to grab my nearly empty pack. Victoria came around the corner and peeked at the strange man standing outside. He walked right past her and into my kitchen, which was definitely not okay.

"You still have pills?" He pointed at the windowsill where I'd put them.

"Um, yeah," I told him, trying to escort him back outside. Maybe I felt guilty about having them, but there was no way he was getting my pills. I'd already slipped back into that addict mentality of hoarding my drugs. The nightmare was happening all over again. I cursed the old lady for not giving me an aspirin in the first place, forgetting I was the one who had asked her and not the other way around.

After I put Victoria to bed, I sat outside in the night sky and tried to figure everything out. There was no way I could still afford to live in my awesome duplex with no job. Rent was also due soon, and I'd already spent part of the money on drugs.

Even if I could stall for a few days, I had no way now of coming up with what I needed. Not to mention the addict who now thought it was okay to show up at my door anytime he wanted. It was only a matter of time before he would ask me to drive him to get more drugs, and I doubted I'd be able to resist. There was also the old pervert across the yard to deal with. Feeling desperate, I called Eric.

"I got laid off," I lied as I worked up a few tears. "I don't know what to do."

"I don't know," Eric sounded irritated. "You could find a rich guy."

I told Eric his joke wasn't funny and hung up the phone feeling completely screwed. There wasn't a single person left who would help me out of this situation. People had been proud of me for doing so well, and I was about to disappoint all of them. Any hint of acting out and especially doing drugs would change their opinions of me forever. Looking for another job would also take time. Even if I found work, my first check wouldn't come for weeks. I felt completely and utterly alone.

There was only one chance to save myself and Victoria, but it was the last thing I wanted to do. I grabbed my phone and dialed, trying to take deep breaths and stop crying.

"I'm coming home."

Chapter Twenty-Six

Micah was waiting for me in his driveway when I pulled up to his apartment building. Walking up to him, I noticed his jaw clenched and spasming. He sounded so excited when I told him I wanted to come back. What was he mad about now?

He guided me and Victoria to the back of the triplex where he was living and ushered me inside. His apartment consisted of a windowless living room, a kitchen with a hot plate, a tiny refrigerator and a small bedroom where a stained mattress lay on the tile floor. It was completely depressing, especially after having left the beautiful duplex in Cape Coral.

I sat down on the mattress and checked my voice messages. There were several from Tim and Nancy wondering where I'd gone. They pleaded with me to let them know I was okay. Still unable to put what happened into words, I didn't call them back. The only person who knew I was back in town was Micah, but surely that would change as soon as Tim got a hold of Eric. I didn't even dare to think what that would be like.

Micah stood over me. "You should know I'm not doing drugs anymore, so don't even think about getting into that. I'm going to AA now."

"I wasn't going to ask," I said weakly. I only half believed Micah was clean and sober. Drinking alcohol was like breathing to him, and he always took any drug he could get his hands on. Self-medicating was the only way he had ever gotten by, and for him to give that up seemed shocking.

"I can't believe you let another man put a needle in your arm," Micah said, repeating the story I told him on the phone. "That's just as bad as cheating."

"I didn't cheat on you, Micah." I insisted. "I don't even know the guy's name. It happened before I could stop it. The whole thing was dumb."

Micah turned away. "Well, just to let you know, that kind of stuff won't fly here. I'm done with that shit."

He hadn't hugged me yet or acted happy to see me. In fact, he seemed almost disgusted with me. I wasn't sure what to do with this new empowered Micah. Maybe I could keep a low profile for a while, as difficult as that was in such a small apartment.

When Micah left for work the next day, I had a full-blown panic attack. The realization of what I'd done hit me full force. What would Eric say when he found out I was back? Would he ever let me see the boys? Was Micah really going to kick me out if I used drugs again? What about losing my job? How was I going to make any money?

I hurried to the nearest convenience store and bought a bottle of wine. It was my way of self-medicating, but I felt desperate and had to get to a state where I could think clearly. Back at the apartment, I drank glass after glass trying to calm myself down. That never happened, but I did end up drunk. The loud buzzing in my body quieted down. Even though I felt guilty for

261

drinking, I was grateful to get some rest. I lay down on Micah's mattress and tried to sleep the anxiety away.

Another transcription company hired me to work from home. I forced myself to sit at my computer and type as much as possible, but I had trouble paying attention. Staying home alone all day with only my thoughts wasn't good for my mental health. It was important to function every day and be a good mother to Victoria. I'd let her down so many times, yet she still looked at me as if I hung the moon. The last thing I wanted to do was let her down again.

Micah kept asking me to go with him to an AA meeting, saying he needed the support. When I agreed to go, he took me to a building tucked back into the woods called Club Oasis. Inside, we were warmly greeted by fellow addicts and alcoholics. We listened to people tell war stories of their life with addiction and how they turned things around with the help of their "higher power." I felt somewhat jealous of those people, living their lives so freely without needing substances to regulate their moods.

They seemed genuinely happy. I thought about my higher power but could only envision one ashamed of me for being so disappointing and stupid.

The AA stories were inspirational, but I couldn't relate to people's awesome lives in sobriety. It all seemed so far out of reach. Micah sat next to me soaking in everything that every person said. He told me later he felt like one of the "chosen ones" who survived his battle with addiction and had the power to help others still suffering.

Micah introduced me to some of his friends after the meeting. It was nice to see him interacting with people in a positive way. For the first time, I felt a little envious of Micah. Alcohol and drugs still had a giant hold over me, and it made me sad that he dared to get help and left me behind.

Two weeks after I returned to town, I finally heard from Eric. As expected, Tim and Nancy had told him about me leaving the West Coast. Eric was furious in a way I'd never experienced before. He blasted me in an email, calling me sick and selfish and a horrible parent. I didn't write him back. There was nothing I could say. I couldn't tell him about my time in Cape Coral. He'd never let me see the boys again. My heart was wrecked from being away from them for so long. I wanted to hug them so much that my arms ached constantly.

I wished I were still at the townhouse letting them sneak into my room in the middle of the night, their little bodies breathing next to mine as I patted their hair, and the way they would wake me up in the morning with a smile and a giggle. It was all getting harder to remember. They didn't deserve a crazy mother like me. I hoped Eric's new girlfriend was reading to them at night and giving them all the hugs they needed. I hoped she truly saw what treasures they were and loved them almost as much as I did.

Micah and I spent our evenings listening to music and eating the dinner he always cooked. He still seemed put off by me, and I resolved to stay out of his way as much as possible. Without him, I knew I'd be homeless. I was lucky that he gave me a place to live; however, I was getting more restless and anxious every day. I still missed the pills and the calming effect they had on me. My anxiety was still prevalent, and I needed something to make it go away.

"You know what would be fun?" I asked Micah one evening after dinner. "If we each had a Roxy, just one, to enjoy our night."

It was cruel and I knew it. He was trying to stay clean, and there I was trying to throw him off the wagon. I couldn't help myself. Ever since my relapse in Cape Coral, getting high was all I could think about.

Micah sighed, "I'm riding my bike up to the gas station," he announced. "If you're lucky, maybe I'll bring you back some beer."

I felt like the dirtiest piece of scum as I watched Micah leave. He was obviously angry with me. I should have never asked him in the first place. Even though Micah contributed to my drug addiction, now I was the bad influence. I tried to lie down and sleep until he got back. Maybe a beer would be all right, something to take the edge off.

I was sound asleep when Micah came back and shook me awake. "Never ask me for this again," he demanded. "I met a guy at the gas station who was selling these, and I got one for each of us."

He held out his hand and displayed the little blue pills that were so familiar. I pinched one out of his palm and agreed it would be the last time. We both knew it was a lie. I took my pill into the bathroom and chopped it up on the tile floor, using a spoon to crush it into blue powder. Then I rolled up a dollar bill and snorted it all. I pressed my finger into the remaining specks, bringing it to my mouth and licking it off. It tasted terrible and like heaven at the same time.

When I came out of the bathroom, Micah was sitting at my computer playing music. I didn't see him take his pill but assumed he did. His mood was brighter as he motioned for me to sit down next to him and listen to his songs. I was glad we were getting along, at least for a few hours. Bless that guy at the gas station and being in the right place at the right time. The opiate effect was soothing and calmed me once again.

"Did you get that guy's phone number?" I asked Micah, instantly forgetting my promise.

"No," he answered. "I didn't ask him for it because we aren't doing this again."

How stupid, I thought. *What if we needed something for a rainy day?* In my world, I constantly waited for the next downpour.

I felt overcome with sadness the next morning once the pill wore off. Was I really never going to see another Roxy again? How was I supposed to function and be productive? I was back in the mindset where I couldn't do any activity without being high, believing I needed pills to work, look after Victoria and clean the apartment. How in the world was I going to do all that without help?

When Micah got home from work, I started in on him. "Why didn't you get that guy's phone number? I can't stop this anxiety on my own. I need something to make it go away."

Micah sighed and rolled his eyes, "God, I can't believe you sometimes. Why do you have to be such a disgusting drug addict? Why can't you control yourself?"

I didn't have an answer to his question. He was right. I let those tiny blue pills take precedence over everything in my life, even my children. My daughter was starving for attention, but I couldn't focus long enough to spend quality time with her. Micah didn't seem to have any interest in her at all. We were so caught up in our own lives that Victoria got left behind.

I enrolled Victoria in a preschool at the end of our street. The staff was sweet with her, so much that I spent what little money I had left for registration and her first two weeks. I wanted her to get the love and attention she needed, and her new teacher seemed happy to oblige. It would be a relief to know she was having fun at least part of the day. Our little windowless apartment was so confining and lonely.

When Micah returned that night, I told him about the school. He seemed uninterested, instead reaching into his pocket and holding his hand out. Inside his palm was what I wanted the most.

"I lied," he admitted. "I got that guy's number. Don't think it will be a regular thing though. Those pills are twenty bucks a pop."

I snatched the pill from Micah and went into the bathroom to snort it. The oxycodone flooded my body instantly. Micah was likely going to be a jerk about it, but I didn't care. The pills gave me life and happiness and everything I thought I needed to live again. I wasn't about to turn that down.

"Feel better?" Micah was being sarcastic, but I pretended not to notice as my fear slipped away.

Micah spoke again, "Hey, I ran into the landlord on the way in. He's getting nasty about us not paying the rent. Do you have money you can contribute?"

I'd spent everything I had on Victoria's school. Micah was enraged, especially since I was home all day and therefore needed no one to watch Victoria. I stood my ground and explained that school was non-negotiable. It was an escape for Victoria of this boring existence. He backed down and couldn't argue with that.

Before long, Micah was bringing me a pill every day that I paid for out of my transcription money. He made it clear he wasn't happy to hand them over. "Why can't you ever buy me a pill?" he sulked. On other nights, however, he sometimes came home excited with a fancy dinner to make for us and a little toy for Victoria.

"I got a bonus at work today," he told me.

It was nice to see him so happy. His new job was in telemarketing, which could be rough sometimes, but at least he was getting bonuses and occasionally making big sales that cheered him up. When that happened, sometimes he would have me buy two pills instead of just one. I never saved them for a rainy day, preferring to snort them as soon as they were in my hand. When we had pills, Micah and I got along great. He didn't call me an unstable drug addict or any of the other mean things he usually said. He acted like he was glad I was there.

There were some nights that Micah couldn't get pills from the dealer. I'd experience withdrawal almost instantly and sob for hours, begging him to try to at least get something for us. Surely the guy from the gas station could get another type of drug.

"I don't want to make him mad," Micah said. "He's already overwhelmed with me asking for pills all the time. He said he needed some for himself."

The last thing I wanted to do was make our drug dealer angry, not when he was my lifeline. Still, I begged Micah to ask for at least half a pill. He left the apartment and didn't come back until late. When he returned, he handed me a Suboxone, telling me it would take the edge off. I saw it as a kind gesture. It seemed like he really did care about me withdrawing and realized

how much I was hurting. I silently thanked
the unseen man from the gas station who
had drugs and would sell them to us cheap.
He was the only thing keeping me going.

Chapter Twenty-Seven

I couldn't remember the last time I'd seen my boys. My heart ached terribly for them every day, and thinking about either one of them would send me on a crying jag for hours. How could I ever face them? They hated me being with Micah as much as I hated it. I had nothing good to share with them about my life.

Before the kids were born, there was so much I wanted to teach them and experience with them. None of that was happening now. I had no hand in raising them anymore and no influence on their lives. Eric's current girlfriend was tucking them in at night and cleaning smudges off their faces and hearing about what happened to them at school. As grateful as I was for a maternal influence in Brandon and Shawn's lives, losing them tore me up inside.

I finally reached out to Eric and asked if I could see them. To my surprise, he agreed. We set up a time for later in the week. Even though the plan excited me, I felt growing anxiety. Would the boys disapprove of me or even hate me? They were older now and more aware of things. It made me sad to realize that I really didn't know them at all anymore. An hour of having lunch at McDonald's wasn't going to change that.

Fate intervened a few days later when I got pulled over by a police officer. He noticed that the tag on my license plate was not current. I'd actually known this for months and been driving around with fear in the pit of my stomach, trying to avoid being spotted. I just didn't have the money to pay for a new tag.

The officer was no-nonsense as he asked for my driver's license, insurance and registration. There would be no charming him or crying for effect. I could tell he meant business. He walked back to his car, and every minute seemed like an hour as I waited for him to come back. I took deep breaths and tried to stop my hands from shaking as I gripped the steering wheel.

"Ma'am," the officer said when he returned. "Did you know your license is suspended?"

I honestly didn't. The officer explained that my license was suspended automatically when I didn't pay for my registration.

"I'm so sorry, I had no idea. What does this mean?"

The officer leaned closer to my window. "Well, it means you can't drive and we have to take your car."

I lowered my head in defeat. There was nothing I could do. The officer waited as I retrieved my personal items from inside the car. We stood together on the side of the road while we waited for the tow truck.

"Look, I hate to do this," he admitted. You seem like a nice lady."

"It's okay." I felt a sudden need to reassure him. "Could you give me a ride home? I only live a few blocks away."

The officer nodded yes as the truck pulled

up. I watched my poor little car get hooked up to the hitch and disappear down the street. When the policeman pulled up to my apartment, I saw Micah looking out the window. He didn't come outside to find out what happened. He was deathly afraid of cops, even when he wasn't doing anything wrong.

"What's going on?" he asked nervously as I walked through the front door.

I explained the situation, including the fact that we didn't have a car now. The officer told me that the fee from the towing company would get higher every day I didn't come pick it up. If that were the case, I would never see it again. I couldn't afford that kind of money.

"How can you be so calm about this?" Micah wanted to know.

I shrugged my shoulders and walked into the other room. Did Micah want me to cry over my car after everything else? I'd come to expect bad things to happen by then. They always did, and it was usually my fault.

None of it fazed me anymore.

I called Eric the next day and let him know I wouldn't be able to come pick up the boys after all. His response was a mixture of anger and disappointment. The thought of letting Brandon and Shawn down again was devastating.

Shortly after Eric and I hung up, my phone rang again. It was Eric's girlfriend, Kathy.

"I heard what happened to your car. I'm so sorry," she told me.

I thanked her, feeling tears welling in my eyes and wiping them away. It would have been weird if she heard me crying. We barely knew each other.

"I was just wondering," she continued, "Do you want me to pick you up so you can see the boys?"

"Oh gosh, are you sure you don't mind?"

"Not at all," Kathy reassured me. "They were very sad at the thought of not getting to meet up with you."

It was such a kind offer. I felt grateful to this woman for caring so much and thanked her repeatedly. We agreed that she would come get me the next day and take me to see Brandon and Shawn. Kathy didn't make me feel embarrassed about it. She seemed happy to help, and I was grateful for her kindness.

Kathy showed up the next morning after Micah went to work. I got Victoria dressed and ready. The boys would be thrilled to see her even if they were upset with me. I'd only met Kathy a few times before. She was young, fit and attractive with a mop of brownish-black hair barely touching her shoulders and large brown eyes. I felt grateful that Eric had found such a nice woman to live with him and the boys.

I let Kathy into the apartment and tried not to notice the surprised look on her face. The little space looked so bad, not just messy but dark and depressing. Kathy looked around, catching Victoria's eye and smiling at her. Victoria's face lit up from the attention she needed so badly. I finished packing us up, and we got into Kathy's little sports car. Victoria was excited about seeing her brothers and sang in the backseat as we pulled out of the driveway.

We were halfway up the block when Kathy suddenly pulled over to the side of the road. She turned to face me in the passenger's seat.

"Do you really want to keep living like this?" she asked me.

The word "no" popped out of my mouth before I could stop it. It felt like it wasn't even me who said it, but someone inside me who was begging for help.

"Brandon and Shawn miss you so much."

I broke out into large shaking sobs. For a long time, I'd let myself believe the boys were better off without me. I pictured them happy with Kathy and Eric and forgetting all about me. Now I realized they remembered everything. It hurt my heart to think how much my absence affected them. I thought their lives were perfect and I was unnecessary.

Kathy put her hand on my arm and spoke gently, "Let's go get your stuff."

"Right now?"

"Yes," Kathy answered. "Right this minute. Put all of this misery behind you."

The same voice inside that said "no" earlier suddenly said "yes" without hesitation. Kathy turned the car around and headed back for the apartment, where I gathered as much stuff as Victoria and I needed. I had no idea where Kathy was taking us, but anywhere was better than the miserable windowless apartment.

I imagined Micah's response when he found out I left him again. He would be angry for sure, but my desire to leave was much stronger than any negative reaction from him. I never wanted to see him or the drugs again. Kathy helped me load everything in her car, and when she drove away I felt a huge burden lift off my shoulders. It was time to heal.

Chapter Twenty-Eight

Kathy drove me to her condo in Jupiter that she rented from Eric. Somewhere along the way of being tenant and landlord, they had developed a romantic relationship. Now they were both living in Eric's house with the boys, and the condo was left empty.

"So you can stay here," Kathy announced as she began to clear space for my things. It sounded like a great idea. The hour was getting late, and I wanted to rest and clear my head. Micah would have gotten home from work already, and my stomach felt nervous thinking about what he would do when he found me gone. I tried to ignore my worries as I helped Kathy clean up.

She worked like a madwoman, frantically scrubbing the counter tops and vacuuming the carpet almost in a violent manner. I wanted to tell her to slow down, but she was on a tear. She showed me all her furniture and told me it could stay in the condo so I could use it. She pointed to her closet, saying that I could wear any clothes she left behind since we were the same size. I couldn't believe how nice she was being and felt guilty about the burden I was putting on her and Eric to give me a place to stay.

Two hours later, Kathy decided the place was clean enough. She slumped on the couch looking exhausted, which only made me feel worse. She didn't need to do all that work. I was just happy to have a home, messy or not, as long as it didn't involve Micah.

"I'm gonna go," Kathy told me as she picked up her purse. She turned to me with a serious look on her face.

"Before I leave, I want you to know something. If you and Eric get back together, I'm totally okay with it."

What? I was in complete shock. Where had she come up with such an idea? There was a less than zero chance that Eric and I would ever reconcile. The very idea of it was laughable. After everything we'd been through, we barely even tolerated each other. I told Kathy she had nothing to worry about, but after she left I wondered what made her say that in the first place. Who would ever be "okay" with an ex-wife stealing their boyfriend?

As expected, Micah came home to an empty apartment that first night and freaked out. When he couldn't gain access to me any other way, he posted terrible lies about me on Facebook. I hoped my real friends wouldn't believe his posts and would remember the truth about me.

After ignoring the harassment for a while, I finally sent him an angry email telling him to stop. Micah threatened to publish nude photos I'd sent him when I still lived in Virginia. He said he would spread them all over the Internet. He was vindictive and angry, and I had no doubt that he would go through with it. Instead of fighting back against his poison, I decided not to write a response at all. I had to stay strong and concentrate on the future, not the past.

Eric and Kathy referred me to a buy-here, pay-here shop where I could get a used car for cheap. If I missed a payment, my car would be repossessed immediately, so I'd have to be extra careful with money. I chose a little white Toyota just big enough for me, Victoria and the boys. The thought of going where I wanted when I wanted again sounded wonderful. I'd even be able to pick up the boys and take them places. Eric and Kathy were being so kind, and I promised myself to make it up to them as soon as I was back on my feet.

Kathy brought Brandon and Shawn over the day after I arrived. The boys were thrilled that I had left Micah and was living so close to them now.   The two of them played on the floor with Victoria while Kathy and I chatted. She asked me questions about how my detox was going. It was the last thing I wanted to talk about. The shame of being an addict was unbearable.

Even though Kathy was doing so much to help me, the truth was I didn't know her well enough yet to confide in her. We sat in silence on her couch as she brushed out Victoria's long strawberry-blonde hair while my little girl chatted and sang to her brothers.

Victoria followed Kathy when she got up to go to the bathroom. Kathy shut the door behind them, and I heard them giggling from the other room. I was happy they were bonding. Maybe it wouldn't be weird to be friends with Eric's girlfriend after all. I hoped Eric wouldn't have a problem with it.

When Victoria emerged from the bathroom a few minutes later, her hair was six inches shorter and cut in a bowl shape around her head. I gasped and jumped up from the couch. What had Kathy done, and why hadn't she asked me first?

"I think it will be easier to manage," Kathy said before I could speak. "Don't you?"

I didn't know what to say. Who cuts a child's hair without asking when their mother is in the next room? Kathy was sticking out her neck for me, but that didn't mean she was in charge of me or Victoria.

Kathy stood with her arms crossed and a defensive look on her face while Victoria twirled around in front of me.

"I look pretty, Mommy?"

I hugged my daughter and told her yes. After all, what did it really matter? Hair always grew back, and making a fuss over it seemed rude after Kathy had been so nice. I decided it was better just to let it go.

After nearly two weeks of staying in the condo, my head was finally straightening out. It was easier to make small goals and meet them without the drugs in my system. I envisioned a life of peace for me and my children where we all lived again under one roof. It seemed like an unreachable dream, but I couldn't give up hope.

Kathy called me late one night when Victoria was asleep. The tone in her voice was strange, like she'd been drinking or something.

"Are you doing drugs, Glenna?" she shouted at me. "Are you clean?"

"Yes," I answered. "I haven't had any type of drug in thirteen days. I'm almost over the detox and feel a little better every day."

Kathy snapped back, "I want you to take a drug test."

I had no idea where her attitude was coming from.   She'd been perfectly nice to me and Victoria ever since the day she rescued me. What was with the sudden change in attitude?

"I can take a drug test," I offered, "but why do you need one?"

Kathy ignored my question. "If you fail the test, I want you to promise to let Eric and me raise Victoria. You need to sign over custody and make it official."

My legs started to give out from under me. What was she talking about? There was no way I was going to sign any kind of paper whether I was clean or not. Maybe I owed Kathy for everything she had done to help me, but the cost of that was not my child.

"Kathy, I don't know why…"

She interrupted me with a loud whisper. "I'm going to put Eric on the phone. You will not tell him of our conversation. You're going to say that you can't handle being clean and need somebody to take care of Victoria."

I heard rustling as Kathy put Eric on the phone. What was I going to say to him? My place to live and my daughter were suddenly in jeopardy. If I didn't go along with Kathy's plan, she'd likely kick me out of the condo whether I signed papers or not. I'd end up homeless with a five-year-old child. Eric already thought I was a piece of trash, and he'd never take my side over his girlfriend's. For a minute, I wondered if I should agree to her terms just to get her off the phone. If she was drunk, maybe she would sober up in the morning and forget all about it.

When Eric finally picked up the phone, it was clear he didn't know what Kathy was talking about. He thought I'd called him and asked me what I wanted.

"Eric," I told him. "I need you not to

repeat what I'm about to say, and I need you to trust me. I mean, I know you don't trust me, but please remember the real Glenna and know that I have no bad intentions toward you. I would not lie to you about something this important." I took a deep breath. "There is something really wrong with Kathy."

I told him the story of what happened a few minutes earlier and what Kathy was demanding. Eric remained silent on the other end of the phone. Did I make a big mistake? I prayed he would understand I wasn't trying to mess up his relationship. If he believed that, all hope was lost.

"Okay," Eric finally said before hanging up. He sounded way too calm considering what I'd just told him. Oh my God, was he repeating it to Kathy right now? Was he going to leave me at her mercy to torture me however she wanted. I didn't have a leg to stand on except the truth, which suddenly seemed flimsy and weak. All I could do was wait.

Eric dropped off Brandon and Shawn the

next morning so they could spend the day with me. I hugged both boys and ushered them inside, staying with Eric out on the patio.

"Are you okay?" I asked him.

Eric sighed and rolled his eyes. He looked totally wiped out, like he hadn't slept all night.

"I broke up with Kathy last night after she called you," he admitted.

Relief flooded my body along with shame. I could tell the breakup was hurting Eric, and I felt responsible for his suffering.

"I'm so sorry, Eric. I didn't mean to cause trouble."

"You're not the one who did."

I leaned in and gave Eric a quick hug. It was the most real conversation we'd had since our divorce. Even after all the drama of splitting up and everything that followed, he still believed in me. I felt incredibly grateful.

"I told Kathy she could stay in my house for a month until she finds a place to go," Eric said. "It might be a mistake, though. She ripped me to shreds in front of the boys last night."

I hated the idea of Brandon and Shawn feeling scared by Eric and Kathy arguing. Hopefully, the month would go by fast.

"Also," Eric continued, "I think it's time for you to find another place to live."

I didn't see it coming, but I wasn't surprised either. Eric needed rent money, and so far I hadn't given him a dime. He needed a real tenant who would pay their bills or else he'd lose money on the condo every month. I was also a lot more trouble than I was worth. Even though I was facing potential homelessness again, I wasn't mad at Eric. At least he gave me some time to find another place.

It was time for me to stop leaning on my ex-husband. He didn't belong to me anymore, and it was best to keep it that way.

Chapter Twenty-Nine

I found a cute cottage for rent in Jupiter
Farms. It was located just five minutes away
from Brandon and Shawn, which was the
whole reason I picked it. The cottage sat
behind a large house that my landlord lived
in with his wife. They seemed like nice and
welcoming people.

The rooms of the cottage were tiny but
charming with wood floors, an upstairs loft,
a small kitchen and a bedroom that Victoria
and I would share. She was thrilled to have
her brothers back in her life and begged to
see them every day. I understood her
excitement. Spending time with the boys was
a salve on my wounded heart.

Driving home one afternoon, I spotted
some wicker furniture that was left on the
side of the road. I had nothing to speak of
except Victoria's portable crib, so I made
several trips in my little car and brought it
all back to the cottage. Finally, we had chairs
to sit in and a table for meals. Victoria and I
sat on the front patio every evening looking

into the darkness at the stars. We lived away from the city, but I found beauty in the silence and the view.

I had a chance to turn my life around and let go of all the toxic things that took over for far too long. I started attending AA meetings regularly on my own and really listened to what the speakers said. Gradually, I found comfort at Club Oasis and started to make a few new friends.

One night in a meeting, I listened to the man up front give his testimony and was blown away by his honesty and his desire to help others now that he'd stopped drinking. His name was Peter, a middle-aged man with silver hair and a friendly smile. I'd never heard the horrors of addiction spoken in such a powerful way mixed in with a message of recovery, and I felt compelled to meet him when he was done and introduce myself.

"I just want to thank you for everything you said tonight," I told him. "You are a wonderful speaker."

Peter seemed touched by my words, and we continued to chat for a moment. He also lived in Jupiter Farms with his wife, Carol, who was in recovery as well. He offered me a ride to the next AA meeting, and I gratefully accepted. Peter seemed to be such a wise person, and I wanted to soak up as much of it as I could. Not only had Peter and Carol conquered their addictions, they had devoted their lives to helping others do the same.

Peter and Carol picked me up two evenings later for the meeting. I liked Carol right away. She was genuine and sweet as she enveloped me in a giant hug. She and Peter listened intently as I opened up about Micah and everything I'd been through. They agreed it would be best not to have any contact with him and ignore his emails calling me selfish, a disgusting addict, a mental case and any other comments designed to make me feel like a loser.

Of course, I should have blocked him a long time ago. They were absolutely right. I was ashamed of how long I'd been reading those emails and sometimes responding out of anger or loneliness. A clean break was sorely needed.

Peter and Carol took me out for sushi after the meeting and picked up the bill. I protested at first, but realized I barely had any money to speak of and couldn't turn down their generosity. They let me talk more during dinner and gave me some gentle advice. I felt grateful that they cared enough to want to help.

I'd never met two people who were as selfless. It became a ritual to spend time at their house, sometimes watching Law and Order reruns and other times talking for hours. My favorite place in the world was their patio with the cushy chairs, candles, plants, and inspirational books on the tables. It felt like home for the first time in a long time.

Sometimes Carol played with Victoria while Peter and I would sit outside for hours talking about recovery. My self-confidence was trashed, but Peter said he saw something special in me. He saw a willingness to get better and to live life as the woman and mother I was supposed to be. Instead of lying to him, I was completely honest with him in a way I'd never been before. Together we figured out ways to get past the pain without numbing myself with drugs and alcohol. He was a firm believer in the twelve steps of AA, telling me it saved lives and gave people a second chance to be happy, joyous and free.

Peter promised he and Carol were going to help me through the program. He also said it was rare that a person actually went all the way through the twelve steps, but he believed I had a chance to make it happen. He cut me the break I couldn't give myself and made me believe I was worthy of a brand new start.

Peter and I got down to work. At his direction, I wrote down names of people who I felt hurt me and people that I hurt. Peter always sent me back to my paper to think of more. He wanted the list to be longer, the writing deeper into myself. I worked like crazy, wanting desperately to reach my goal. The thought of being my true self under all the depression, anxiety and trauma appealed to me, like meeting someone for the first time who I wanted to know better. Peter and Carol fed me dinner, bought me cigarettes and shelled out a little bit of pocket money on occasion. I still hadn't learned to manage my money, so they helped me draw up a budget. They both insisted helping me also helped them. It was the twelfth step, being altruistic and giving comfort and aid to another addict.

I felt a little guilty at the thought of using up Peter and Carol's time and resources. *Why couldn't I do these things myself?* I barely knew how to cook or change a spare tire, and I had no idea how to manage my life. For years, Eric had taken care of everything important. During my time with Micah, I didn't care enough to try anything new at all. I prayed that going through the twelve steps would make me a willing and able person who depended on herself.

I wrote my fourth step earnestly, examining the pivotal incidents that made up my past. I wanted progress as fast as possible. Peter warned me to slow down and give good consideration to each step, but I felt time was of the essence. There were already signs of my depression lurking in the background. On the nights I didn't visit Peter and Carol, the cottage began to feel like a prison. I had Victoria with me but still felt isolated.

There was no man to love and share my life with for the first time since I was fifteen years old. It felt uncomfortable and weird. I couldn't expect my new friends to include me fully in their lives, but being alone felt dangerous. I didn't yet trust myself to make good choices on my own. I was 40 years old and still felt lost without another person around to guide me.

That was when I started reading Micah's emails again. He still sent them almost every day, and they were always mean. He attacked every weak spot where I was vulnerable. He tried to manipulate me as usual into feeling guilty for leaving him, but there was something else. Underneath his anger, I realized he was even more lonely than me. As the messages progressed, he wrote that he still loved me and missed me all the time. I kept reading when I knew I

shouldn't, making sure to conceal it from
Peter. I knew I was playing with fire and
didn't want him to be disappointed in me.

Micah kept saying he missed Victoria, and
I felt guilty for keeping her away from her
father. He wanted to see her badly, so I
agreed to pick him up at his apartment and
bring him to the cottage for the afternoon.
He said his place was not good for children,
and I couldn't argue with that.

Micah insisted on riding in the back seat
with Victoria and giggled with her the whole
way. I stayed quiet as the two of them
chatted all the way to Jupiter Farms. Had I
misjudged him? Did he really care about
Victoria and want to be a part of her life?

Back at the cottage, I made lunch for all of
us while Micah commented on where I was
living. "Moving on down, I see," he said
with an eye roll. I knew he was joking, but
it still stung. I'd tried to make a nice home
for Victoria and suddenly doubted whether
I'd succeeded. When I brought Micah his
plate of food, he took me by the arms and
kissed me. *I don't want this*, I tried to

convince myself, but I let loneliness get the best of me. During Victoria's nap on the couch, Micah and I went in the bedroom. I'd forgotten what human contact was like and how much I missed it. *Nobody will ever find out*, I decided. I'd never tell other people what I'd done.

When Victoria woke up, we drove Micah back to his apartment. The shame I felt was overwhelming. I was certain I never wanted sex with Micah to happen again, no matter how nice he was being to me and Victoria.

"Why don't you pick me up on Friday to stay for the weekend?" Micah asked as I pulled up to the curb.

"I can't do that." I said weakly.

"Why not?"

I sighed and continued. "Because this was a mistake, Micah. I don't want to get into a thing with you all over again."

Micah's eyes widened. "But you slept with me and now it means nothing? I know you still have feelings for me."

"It doesn't matter what my feelings are. It's what's best for me and my children. Anytime we try to reconcile it's a toxic disaster."

I could see the hurt on Micah's face and felt bad about having caused it. It never occurred to me that it wasn't "just sex" for Micah. My desperation for some kind of connection made me impulsive, but now I'd hurt him in the process. How could I be so selfish?

"It's okay."   Micah waved his hand in front of my face to punctuate brushing me off.   "You should know there are a lot of women who find me attractive and want to spend time with me. I guess I'll take them up on their offers."

My face felt hot as he issued the threat. Whether Micah and I were together or apart, there had never been anyone else in the picture. The thought of Micah sleeping with another woman made me feel sick to my stomach.   Even though I didn't really want him for myself, it hurt that there were other girls who did.

Micah shrugged his shoulders. "Whatever. It's better this way. At least now I don't have to share my pills."

"What are you talking about?"

Micah laughed in my face. "All those pills you paid me for were from my own prescription. I got a storage locker not too far from the apartment so I could hide them."

"So there's no drug dealer guy from the gas station?"

"Nope," Micah answered proudly. "I fill my prescription every month, sell half to my friend and take the other half for myself. Well, I did until you came along. I got sick of sharing with you."

My heart sank. The whole "guy with the pills" story was a lie that Micah told me day after day. I felt like the most stupid person in the world. Every time Micah threatened that "the guy" was getting angry about selling

his pills, it was only Micah worrying about
his own stash. He took my money and
pocketed it, all while telling me what a loser
I was for buying drugs in the first place. The
AA meetings he went to were all bullshit.
He'd been using the whole time.

Micah got out of the car.   "I hope you
know what you're doing," he said as he
leaned into the open car window.

"I don't know you," I told him.

It was the truth. Nobody who claimed to
love me would have tricked me like that. He
said he was ready to move on with someone
else. Good for him! I never wanted to see
him again.

Chapter Thirty

I saw Peter a few nights later and didn't mention my afternoon with Micah. Peter knew something was wrong even though I insisted I was fine. I knew he would be so disappointed in me. There was no way I could tell him the truth.

I wanted to get back on track with the twelve steps and forget everything that happened, except I couldn't forget the threat Micah made to sleep with somebody else. The cottage seemed to crush me during the nights I was alone obsessing over other women. Micah made me feel special, even when he was horrible, and the thought of him charming another girl out of her clothing was eating me alive.

It was around this time that I got an email from Mark, the mailman I'd been casually seeing before I went to Virginia. I filled him in on everything that happened when I was there. He was sympathetic and wanted to know if we could get together. I invited him to stop by the cottage. Victoria was thrilled to have her old friend back, and Mark was excited to see her again. Although I wasn't madly in love with him, sometimes I wondered what it would be like to build a future with him. The thought of a stable life sounded appealing, and he made it clear that was what he wanted. Maybe I could learn to love him.

The next time I invited Mark over, we were sitting outside on my patio when I noticed he was looking at my ashtray. I'd started smoking again after Victoria was born. Mark didn't smoke, but for some reason he was staring at the ashtray on the table like he was trying to figure something out.

"The butts," he finally said.

"What?"

Mark pointed to the ashtray. "Some of those cigarette butts aren't yours."

When I looked, I noticed Micah's cigarettes mixed in with mine. Damn, why didn't I empty the ashtrays before Mark came over? I didn't even think of it.

I thought about lying to Mark and saying a girlfriend had come over and smoked on my porch. The lie was on the tip of my tongue, but I couldn't bring myself to say it. Mark knew all about what I'd been through with Micah, but he didn't realize how intertwined Micah and I still were. I didn't yet have the power to shut him out of my life, and Micah never stopped looking for a way in. It wasn't fair to Mark to lead him on.

"I think you should go," I told Mark. "You need to get away from me and forget I even exist."

It was harsh but necessary. Mark deserved better than a girlfriend still hung up on somebody else. He should have a woman who loved him for real.

"Okay," Mark said, standing up to leave. I wanted to call after him to ask him to stay, but I knew I shouldn't. A clean break was the best thing.

Mark paused in my doorway and turned around to look at me. "I love you, Glenna. I could have given you a normal life," he said in a sad voice.

I had no doubt that Mark could have tried to make my life better, but he needed to know he wasn't dealing with a "normal" person. I was far too toxic for picket fences and happily ever after, and I hoped one day he'd find somebody who worshiped him. He was a genuinely good guy.

Soon after Mark and I broke up, I fell into a deep depression, not wanting to leave the cottage even as it stifled me. Peter and Carol asked me to go to meetings, but I told them I wasn't feeling well. "It's just for this week," I lied. "When I'm better, I'll definitely come with you."

The depression wasn't just situational; it was also chemical. I didn't have the money to pay for my bipolar medications and was afraid to tell anybody. Any sense of stability vanished after two days without them, and I felt highly anxious and depressed at the same time. There was no way I could pay for the three medicines I needed until my next paycheck. How was I supposed to earn any money at all to buy them if I wasn't well enough to type? Every day, my mental health got a little worse, and I was afraid of how bad it would get until I could treat it again.

I wanted to forget everything and feel numb. Feelings were too painful to deal with. I found myself in a liquor store buying a bottle of rum and some Coke, just this one time, so I didn't have to feel anything for a while. The cottage seemed to get more confining every day.

I tortured myself with negative thoughts about what a loser I was while ruminating about the bad things I'd done since Eric left me. I'd failed as a wife, a mother and a human being. I deserved to live a life of isolation. The enthusiasm I once had for the AA program was lost, and instead I spent my nights lying in bed with the TV on but not watching it.

That was when I had the first stirrings about killing myself. It wasn't the same as the attention-seeking suicide I'd attempted to get Eric to notice me during our divorce. This time, the thoughts rolled around in my mind and wouldn't let go, urging me to follow through. After all, my children didn't need a mother like me. People were right when they called me unstable. All I ever did was let everyone down and hurt them. The only thing that kept me going was the thought that it would all be over soon. I'd just go to sleep and never wake up. Nobody in their right mind would miss me.

I watched Victoria sleeping in her bed. *I've put her through so much.* A well of tears sprang to my tired eyes. Victoria was still a young girl, but she'd already lived through a lifetime of tragedy that was sure to continue with me as her mother. I just couldn't pretend anymore that I was making a new start for the two of us. I'd used up my nine lives, and I was tired of fighting everyone including myself.

I thought about logistics. Who would look after Victoria after I was gone? She deserved much more than another bad situation. I called my childhood friend, Susan, to ask her what she thought. She was always the type of person who would give it to me straight. She would tell me later that I sounded dead serious and calm about killing myself. Susan answered my questions for a few minutes to keep me on the phone. After we hung up, she called the Jupiter police.

I was sitting on my front patio smoking a cigarette when the officer pulled into my driveway. He asked me if I was okay, and I didn't try to hide my intentions. It was already a done deal in my mind. The cop listened and seemed sympathetic. He suggested taking me to the hospital, but I refused.

"I can't do that," I told him. "I have nobody to look after my daughter."

The cop tilted his head as if he were confused. "Where is her father?"

"He won't take care of her. I know he won't."

"He has to," the officer insisted. "He is her legal guardian and is responsible for her."

Micah couldn't even take care of himself, but the more I talked to the policeman, the more I realized that I was in no condition to care for Victoria either. I wasn't making good decisions because I wasn't in my right mind. The officer didn't shame me for being a bad parent. Instead, he offered comfort and understanding. My first thought was that I didn't deserve his kindness.

"Give me her father's number," he insisted. "I'll talk to him."

I gave the cop the number and sat back down in my wicker chair feeling dead although I was still alive. My main concern was Victoria. I wanted her to be happy with people who truly loved her and didn't think for a second about their own selfish needs.

After about half an hour, a white work truck pulled up to the cottage. It was Micah's boss with Micah in the passenger's seat. I watched as Micah approached the policeman and they talked about me. When they were done, Micah walked past me into the cottage with a nasty look on his face. I knew the cop had given him no choice but to take Victoria. Micah grabbed Victoria's car seat and a few other things I'd gathered up for her ahead of time.

I knelt down before my daughter and gave her a tight hug. "Mommy's going to get help," I told her. "We'll be together again soon."

Victoria didn't protest at all. I'm sure she realized I was not the mother she knew. I didn't look at Micah as he took her little hand. He was furious and I knew it. He buckled our daughter into his boss's truck and didn't look back as they drove away.

After they left, I grabbed my purse and went with the officer to the hospital. We talked on the way there, but most of what he said was a blur. I focused on the sound of his calm voice to stop from crying. This time, I wasn't afraid of the hospital. I realized it was where I needed to be. The cop walked me inside the building and found a nurse to check me in.

With my head still down, I reached out my

arms and hugged the officer who saved my life. "Thank you," I said in all sincerity.

The officer hugged me back. "It's gonna be okay now," he told me. I couldn't remember his name, but I knew I would never forget him.

My new doctor adjusted my medications during my stay on the ward, and I felt a little more lucid with each day that passed. My desperation to go home increased the more I thought about Victoria in Micah's care. Was he being kind and patient with her? I knew Micah loved his daughter, but I wasn't sure he knew how to function as a parent. Even at my worst, I always made sure Victoria's physical needs were met. Could he be trusted to do the same?

I finally called him once I was allowed to use the phone at the nurses' station. His tone was clipped as if he were holding back the enormous rage he felt against me. When I asked about Victoria, he told me his sister Bonnie picked her up the day I went into the hospital.

"But Bonnie lives in Orlando," I said. "Why did you let her go all the way up there?"

"Well, you're obviously useless," Micah answered. I imagined him smirking on his end of the line. "You screwed up and everybody is mad at you. I'm the good one now."

I hung up on him and burst out crying, prompting the nurses to lead me back to my room so I wouldn't upset the other patients. How could Micah have done this? Why couldn't he have watched Victoria for a short couple of days until my release? I hardly knew Bonnie at all. Most of Micah's family turned their back on him long ago, but suddenly his sister was an ally? I imagined going back to the cottage without my daughter. It was almost as if she'd been stolen from me, and I wasn't sure if I could handle it.

Once I was discharged from the hospital, I called Micah back and asked for Bonnie's phone number. He gave it to me without asking questions or wondering if I was okay, but there was no time to be upset about that. I called Bonnie right after I hung up with him and asked when she would bring back my daughter.

"Glenna, she's been through so much already," Bonnie responded. "You just got out of the hospital. Victoria deserves a stable household. Until you can provide her with one, wouldn't it be better if she stayed with me?"

I didn't have an answer. My legs felt like jelly underneath me as I thanked Bonnie for taking care of my daughter. She was right. Victoria deserved better than a mother with mental problems and a pending eviction notice. How could I think I was capable of being a good mom? Bonnie had a husband and a nice house with an extra bedroom for Victoria. It would only be for a little while, until I got things back in order.

"Call Victoria anytime you want," Bonnie offered. "She'd love to talk to you."

I hung up feeling beaten. Cheryl's prediction in Virginia had come true. I was a mother with no children who failed at the most important job she would ever have. Giant wrecking sobs overtook me as I knelt down on the cottage floor. I'd never been so exhausted in my life. When I wore myself out crying, I climbed into my bed where I slept soundly for the rest of the day as if the pain wouldn't be there tomorrow.

When I woke up, the shame I felt for even thinking about suicide was overwhelming. What a horrible thing it would have been to do to my children. Maybe I couldn't pull myself out of my depression, but I didn't have to drag my kids down with me. I didn't love myself, far from it, but I loved them more than life itself. My arms ached for all three of them, but maybe it wasn't too late. I could make Brandon, Shawn and Victoria my sole focus going forward and become the mother they needed.

I had to get better as soon as possible, so I could have them back in my life for good.

Chapter Thirty-One

The weeks that Victoria was supposed to be with Bonnie turned into months. I spent much of the time beating myself up and feeling sorry for myself. *You let your daughter go,* my inner voice taunted, *and it's not like you even see the boys who still live near you. You're a horrible parent and don't deserve children.*

Although I wasn't exactly religious, I prayed every night for Victoria to come home. My prayers always included the boys. I wanted them to be happy even if it meant not having me. I never prayed for myself, believing I didn't deserve it. I felt too lost even for God.

While driving one day, I noticed the new Christian church in the Farms right next to where the kids had gone to preschool. Sometimes I wondered about it when I drove past. Would I ever be welcome in a community that looked down on sinners? Could I find mercy and redemption there?

317

One morning, something told me to drive into the church parking lot. I sat for a while in my car, trying to decide whether to go inside. The idea of talking to someone terrified me, but I needed guidance more than I was afraid.

I turned my car off and went in through the front door. There wasn't a service going on, but maybe I could find an understanding soul. A man waved at me from the other end of the long hallway. I waved back meekly and stood frozen in my spot until he approached me, still not sure what I was going to say.

"Can I help you with something?" He looked like a kind man, maybe in his early thirties, wearing jeans and a dress shirt. He towered over me as he stretched out his arm to shake my hand.

"I'm not sure," I answered. "I think I need to talk to somebody."

"Well, I'm David. Do you want to sit in the conference room?"

I followed David into a large room with a rectangular desk and several office chairs. As I took a seat, I felt tears rising behind my eyes. *Damn it! Don't let me start blubbering.*

"I'm afraid I'll never see my daughter again."

David looked concerned as he moved his chair closer to mine. "Why do you think that?"

"Because my life is a mess," I told him. "I'm about to be evicted and homeless. I have mental health issues that screw everything up, and I can't afford my medication. I left my husband because he was abusive and made me miserable, but things aren't getting any better. I can't stop making bad decisions. I'm not sure where to turn. I don't think God hates me, but everyone else does and I don't know how to fix it."

For a minute, I thought David would encourage me to go back to Micah and try to work things out. Didn't the church frown on divorce? Instead, David excused himself from the room without saying a word. Was I in trouble? Was he going to kick me out?

When David returned, he held two plastic cards in his hand. One was a gift card for the local grocery store, and the other was for gas. It was embarrassing to be given a handout, but I wasn't in a position where I could turn it down.

"Thank you so much," I told him. "I don't know how to repay you."

David smiled. "I was thinking maybe the church could help with your medications, rent this month and a few more gift cards in exchange for you doing some work around here."

I jumped at the chance. The last thing I wanted was to be in debt to his church. Now I could repay them for their help. For the first time in weeks, I felt a spark of hope. If David was willing to fight for me, maybe I could fight for myself.

"What's your relationship with God?"

David asked in a friendly voice.

"My parents were never religious, so I don't know much about Him. I have read parts of the Bible, but I'm not sure yet what I believe."

David smiled. "We have services every Sunday morning if you'd like to come."

"I'd love to."

I drove straight to the pharmacy to get my prescriptions filled, surprised by my own happiness. Not only did the church help me, but they believed in me enough to hire me. I could work at the church in the morning and still transcribe for my shift in the afternoon. It was almost like fate or maybe a message from God. Either way, I looked forward to spending more time at the church. Maybe the goodness would rub off on me.

My first morning there, I helped repaint the outside of the building. The next day, I stuffed the brochures they handed out on Sundays. After that, I worked in the cafeteria where they sold juice and pastries. Every day was something different. On Sundays, I attended the services. It turned out David was the church pastor. He talked about the ways God can work in your life even when you feel powerless. I wondered if going to the church that first day was God trying to guide me. Maybe he was on my side.

Micah still sent me emails every day that brought me back down to Earth. Sometimes he gloated. Other times he said he missed me. I looked forward to the messages in a strange masochistic way. He could never shame me more than I did to myself, but his words reinforced my belief that I was a piece of shit. If I ever forgot, I had Micah to remind me. There was nothing he enjoyed more than kicking me when I was down.

Rent came due and the church helped me pay for it. It made my cranky landlord temporarily happy, but I was already worried about next month. My time with the church was coming to an end. They helped me get back on my feet, but understandably couldn't keep carrying me. David said I was still welcome to come for the services, and I promised him I would. The thought of being on my own again without a purpose scared me. What if I failed and broke down for the hundredth time? What would I have to fall back on?

The fear I had of moving on was enough to paralyze me. I holed myself up in the cottage. Depression nipped at my heels. I felt it coming on strong. I decided not to invite Brandon and Shawn to visit me because I didn't want my mood to scare them. Plus, they'd ask me about Victoria and when she was coming back. I didn't have an answer for that yet.

The friends I'd made in AA faded away, including Peter and Kathy. If they called me, I either pretended I was fine or didn't answer the phone at all. They didn't need to hear that I was drinking every day again. It would only disappoint them, and I couldn't deal with any more promises about getting clean and sober.

I suffered from painful hangovers that left my hands shaking and my head pounding, but I couldn't talk to anyone about it. I told myself it didn't matter. Those AA people weren't real friends unless you were sober. A real friend stuck around during challenging times and didn't abandon you. Framing them in that light made it hurt less, even though they were only cutting me off to protect themselves.

I called Victoria a handful of times. She always asked me in her squeaky little voice when she could come home, and it never failed to break me. When Bonnie got on the phone to check on me, I told her I was fine and hung up. Thanking her for taking care of Victoria seemed impossible. Then I'd have to admit she was really gone.

"I don't care about the bad things you did," Micah wrote in his emails. "I can't stop myself from loving you." He told me he understood me better than I understood myself. He said he loved me when nobody else did.

Micah wanted to make a plan to get Victoria back so we could live as a family. His words became like a water source, a light in the darkness connecting me to the rest of the world. I couldn't get Victoria back on my own, but maybe I could with Micah's help. After all, we were still married, and I'd failed at providing for her on my own. I couldn't stay depressed forever and do nothing about it.

Writing back and forth with Micah about our daughter seemed productive and gave me hope for a future with Victoria in it. He said we were Victoria's legal parents and believed we had every right to live with her again.

Sadly, we didn't stop to think about what Victoria needed or wanted. I was so desperate to have her back that I ignored the fact that her life was more stable than it had ever been with me.

Chapter Thirty-Two

At the end of the summer, I moved out of the cottage and back into Micah's apartment. I still owed my landlord a few hundred dollars but offered to pay him back in installments. He agreed and seemed happy to have me gone, which I understood. I was a liability who couldn't be trusted.

Micah still lived in the sketchy neighborhood rife with drug dealers. His apartment was an even worse disaster than when I left, and I couldn't imagine a child living there anymore. When we got Victoria back, we'd definitely have to move to a safer place. There was no way she could play out in front of the building with her toys, and I doubted there were any other children her age around. I'd have to start saving right away for a new apartment. It had to be my main priority. Micah was paying half the rent, and I would work as hard as I could for extra money to put away.

Micah and I were cautious around each

other, knowing how easy it was for our relationship to blow up like before. It felt like a business arrangement, the two of us teaming up for the sake of our daughter. My love for him had long since passed. I suspected he felt the same, but we seemed destined to be bound together for the rest of our lives. Neither one of us could let go of the other despite the unholy combination.

Both of us were drinking alcohol every day, which made a dent into the Victoria fund. Alcohol was medicine to soothe the pain that threatened to destroy me. Marijuana practically fell out of the sky in our neighborhood, and soon it became part of our evening ritual. I was numbed out, and that was the way I preferred it. It scared me to think the floodgates would open if I dared to let myself think about Brandon, Shawn and Victoria. I couldn't risk it.

Micah was still fond of getting drunk and playing music at an ear-splitting volume. He stomped on the floor with his boots on the tile as he sang along to Motley Crue and Ratt. I begged him to stop making so much noise because we lived on the second floor of the building with a little old lady's apartment underneath us. Micah didn't seem to care and turned his songs up even louder.

"We're not doing anything wrong," Micah said as he took me in his arms to dance with him. It surprised me that the old lady never complained or called the police. Maybe she was hard of hearing?

One Sunday morning, I woke up in the middle of a terrible migraine. I thought at first it was a hangover, but my right temple felt like someone was stabbing it with a knife, my stomach was queasy and my eyes were sensitive to light. When Micah woke up, he rolled his eyes when I told him I was in severe pain. "So what," he said. "I'm hungover every day, but you don't hear me complaining."

I checked my purse for Excedrin and came up empty. Walking to the convenient store the next block over was out of the question. I couldn't even get out of bed.

"I should ask that old lady downstairs if she has any Excedrin for you," Micah offered, trying to be helpful.

I didn't say no or try to discourage him. If I didn't get some relief soon, the rest of my day would be shot. What would this lady think of Micah standing at her door with eyeliner smeared under his eyes from partying the night before? The idea of her reaction made me giggle a little through my pain. Micah was many things, but boring wasn't one of them.

Micah returned a few minutes later with a closed fist and a smile.

"Did she have it?"

"Yeah," Micah said as he opened his hand and revealed three pills instead of just one. "She also sells Dilaudid for five dollars each. I got us some."

"Maybe that's not a good idea," I said as I took one of the pills and swallowed it.

My migraine dissipated within ten minutes. While I was grateful for the relief, I felt bad for taking the pill. It shocked me that

Micah had just scored drugs from a sweet little old lady. I soon fell into an opiate high and forgot all about it. She was an angel as far as I was concerned. Why couldn't I always feel this amazing?

After the day with the Dilaudid, Victoria's "coming home" fund became depleted as we spent all of it on the old lady's pills. The first time I went with Micah to buy pills from her, she greeted me warmly and shook my hand. She said her name was Cookie. I watched as she rummaged through her bag to find her bottle of pills for us as if it was no big deal. When she handed them to Micah, I got a closer look at her face. Her eyes seemed dead to me, as if life had been cruel to her and left her broken, bitter and angry. In that moment, I became afraid of her.

Cookie's generosity in selling us her pills was short lived. "I have pain, too," she complained when we asked her for more. Micah and I pretended to care, but our demand was already too great to leave her alone. We knocked on her door as if our lives depended on it. Cookie only answered half the time no matter how hard we tried.

One afternoon, Micah went to Cookie's apartment and didn't come back for almost an hour. When he finally returned, he had a big grin on his face. He also seemed higher than hell.

"You have to try shooting the Dilaudid," he announced. "Cookie just did it to me and it's awesome."

"I'm not doing that," I told him. *Was he crazy?* The last thing I wanted to do was get involved with needles again. I got a mental image of Cookie in her tiny kitchen with a lighter under a spoon and then injecting Micah's arm with drugs. It seemed bizarre, and I wanted no part of it.

"Cookie used to be a nurse," Micah explained. "She's really good at finding a vein."

"Where did the needle come from?"

"She's a diabetic," Micah said as if he couldn't believe his good fortune. "She's got like a billion needles with each one wrapped in plastic, so it's totally safe."

"I'll just stick with pills," I told him. "A needle would be way too much."

The next time Micah and I visited Cookie's apartment, she came out of her bedroom with two new needles in her hand. Before I could say anything, she took two pills out of her purse and crushed the first one, which she put on a spoon with a little water. Then she held a lighter underneath the spoon for a minute and then drew the liquid up into the syringe. The ritual was fascinating to watch. Cookie seemed to know what she was doing, and I wondered how many times she'd injected people before since her nursing career.

Micah extended his arm, and Cookie tapped on it trying to find a good vein. Then she slid the needle under his skin and deployed the plunger. Micah's eyes immediately rolled back in his head as he smiled at me.

"It doesn't last as long as the pills, but you get so much higher," he slurred.

I saw Cookie about to crush the second pill and stopped her. "No, thank you," I said politely.

"Oh, this ain't for you, honey," Cookie scoffed as she repeated the ritual on herself that she performed for Micah. Her body shook slightly as she injected her right breast. She explained her veins weren't as good as Micah's, so she had to improvise. The living room was silent for a while as Cookie and Micah enjoyed their high. I sat on the couch and watched them, jealous of how euphoric they felt.

"You really need to try this," Micah said, breaking the silence.

"Okay."

It was as if my voice spoke the word without my mind forming the thought first. I hadn't come to Cookie's apartment with the intention of shooting up, but once I had the impulse I couldn't stop myself. The Dilaudid in pill form wasn't getting me as high anymore, as I'd built up a tolerance. I really wanted that feeling again, that sense of floating above all my problems without a care in the world.

   I held my arm out for Cookie and tried to stop it from trembling. It occurred to me that I barely knew this woman, yet here I was letting her inject drugs into my body. I didn't even like Cookie all that much. She gave me the creeps, but I pushed that thought aside because she had what I wanted, an escape from my own mind.

   A warm wave of tingling spread from the left side of my body to the right, and my brain felt all lit up. Micah was right, this was so much better than taking pills. Leaning back on Cookie's couch, I closed my eyes as she talked to Micah at the kitchen table. I didn't care what they were saying. My anxiety and pain were dissolving into dust. Everything that continuously tore me up inside was gone.

   Micah was correct that the high didn't last very long. By the time we got back upstairs to our apartment, I no longer felt like I was in heaven. I grabbed my wallet from my purse and counted out my cash. Since I'd recently been paid, I could afford to get high over and over again at five dollars a pop. It didn't matter how I felt about Cookie. She held the key to my peace of mind. I'd show up at her door every day begging if necessary. The payoff would be worth it.

Micah and I definitely weren't rolling in money, so sometimes we gave up meals to afford Cookie's drugs. When we ran out of cigarettes, Micah sent me to the grocery store to pick through their ashtrays for half-smoked ones. I tried to do this in the morning when nobody would see, but sometimes I'd run into a customer or security guard. When that happened, I put my head down farther and kept picking. It felt like being worlds apart from the way normal people lived, the ones who held their heads up high.

Cookie was a stickler about being paid, refusing to answer her door on days we didn't have cash. I'd bang on it once every hour and plead with her to open it, swearing I'd pay her back and maybe even extra money for her trouble. I kept my voice low so the other neighbors didn't hear me. I cried and begged for her to show me mercy, but Cookie had none. I grew to hate how much I depended on her.

"Cookie, I have money," were the magic words that opened the door between me and the pills. Cookie appeared smiling in the doorway as if she hadn't listened to me weeping and knocking for days. She told me she was tired. She said she never signed up to be a drug dealer and was sick of having to inject me and Micah all the time. Our demands were relentless, and she couldn't keep up with them. I realized Micah and I would have to be careful so we didn't alienate her altogether.

During the days when Cookie sent us away with nothing, Micah and I lay in bed suffering from opiate withdrawal. My body was racked with pain, and I rolled from side to side trying to find some comfort. Micah and I didn't speak to each other because it hurt to move our mouths. The touch of another person was like a hot poker. Neither of us could sleep, so we lay next to each other waiting for the moment when Cookie would call us and invite us over. Sometimes it didn't happen for a week. I couldn't sit at the computer and work anymore without being high, and my paychecks suffered as I typed fewer lines. My belief that I couldn't work unless I was high was unshakable. When Micah tried to force me to sit in my office chair, I cried and refused.

The next time my paycheck came, I didn't share it with Micah. So far, I'd been supporting both of our habits. Micah expected me to do the same again, but I resented him for cutting into Cookie's pill bottle. It was selfish to let him suffer and writhe in the agony of withdrawal, but I felt like I didn't owe him a damned thing.

While he napped, I'd visit Cookie and have her shoot me up as fast as possible before he woke up. I tried to hide the fact that I was high when I returned to the apartment, but Micah got angry when he saw me up and around and being productive.

"How could you?" he wanted to know. I denied it at first, but when he looked into my eyes, he saw my pinpoint pupils and knew I was lying.

"Why don't you get a job and buy your own?" I shot back.

It was mean of me to say, but I felt zero remorse. Micah's boss had fired him a few months earlier for being late too often, and he hadn't been able to find work since then. After everything we'd been through, I felt myself starting to hate Micah. He was the reflection of everything I'd become. We were both junkies and not hiding it very well. The only person we spent any time with was Cookie.

I hadn't seen Brandon and Shawn for months, and the money we saved for Victoria was long gone. The thought of never seeing my daughter again broke my heart, but I felt too helpless to do anything about it. The shame was far too much to bear. I knew Victoria was growing up happy with Bonnie and her husband. I didn't want to swoop in and disrupt her life again when I had nothing to offer. I decided it was better not to feel anything at all.

338

One afternoon I was in Cookie's apartment with my arm outstretched. She seemed nervous when I knocked, first asking if Micah was with me. She took a deep breath when I said he wasn't and let me in.

"Look, I'll still do this for you sometimes," she told me as she reached into her purse for the pill bottle, "but I will never allow Micah in my home again. He has crossed the line."

"What happened?" I asked. As far as I knew, Micah was sleeping in bed where he'd been all day.

Cookie reached for her phone, pushed a few buttons and handed it to me. Micah's voice was suddenly in my ear, but I didn't recognize it right away. He was usually loud and boisterous when he talked, but now he was speaking with a quiet rage that I didn't understand.

"You are not to give Glenna any more drugs without me," Micah threatened on the recording. "You can't give them to her and

not give them to me. I'll ruin you, you old
bitch. I can make you wish you'd never been
born."

I looked up at Cookie, who was still
shaking and upset as she listened along with
me. She was truly scared of Micah. I tried to
reassure her that he was too much of a wimp
to actually do anything about his anger, but I
didn't suggest she share her drugs with him.
I wanted them all for myself.

I went back upstairs and waited for Micah
to wake up, standing over him until he
opened his eyes. He gave me a confused
look.

"What the hell are you doing threatening
Cookie?" I shouted at him. "We will all get
into a lot of trouble if we ever get caught, so
you need to keep your mouth shut."

Micah pushed past me to get to the
bathroom as I followed and continued to yell
at him for screwing up our arrangement.

"Cookie's all freaked out that you're going
to hurt her. She's about to cut both of us off."

"I'm already cut off," Micah said. "You have money and you're not sharing with me anymore.   You know I haven't been able to find work."

"Yeah, I don't think any job recruiters are going to come looking for you in our bedroom."

It was insulting even if it were true. Micah hadn't been on an interview in several weeks. I felt sorry for him, knowing his withdrawal symptoms rendered him incapable of handling his business, but the part of me who hated him now didn't feel bad at all and thought he deserved it.

"I just need to do it one time," Micah begged.   "It will make everything better. I promise."

I turned my back and started to walk away, but Micah grabbed me roughly by the arm and yanked me back into the bathroom.

"You can't do this to me!" He was screaming desperately in my ear, and suddenly I knew why Cookie was afraid of him.

"Better let me go or I'm out of here permanently!" I tried to sound tough, but the furious look on Micah's face had me too paralyzed to move.

It was the wrong thing to say. Micah suddenly dug his fingers into my arm and shoved me down onto the bare linoleum floor. In a flash, he jumped on top of me and pinned me down.

"You're not going anywhere," he insisted, holding me down while I struggled.

"Get your filthy hands off me. You're hurting me!"

Micah's face changed after I said that. He backed off and let me up off the floor. We stood facing each other for a few minutes without speaking. He looked like a broken man who had just realized he was way too old to act this way. He had the exhaustion of the weight of the world in his eyes.

I gathered plastic bags from under the sink and started stuffing my clothes in them randomly. Then I threw all my toiletries into my makeup case. There was nothing else I owned anymore, not a chair or a single fork or anything, but I wasn't worried about material things. I'd already been stripped to my core.

Nudging Micah out of the way, I headed for the front door.

"I'm not a monster, Glenna," he said as tears welled in his eyes. "I'm your husband who loves you."

My answer was to open the door and walk through it, closing it behind me for the last time.

Chapter Thirty-Three

There was nothing left for either of us to say. I felt Micah's power over me dissipate as I walked down the stairs and toward Cookie's apartment. She sighed loudly when she opened the door. I was bothering her again, but I had no choice.

"I'm proud of you," she said when I told her about Micah. "That man is no good."

I relaxed as she plunged a needle into my arm and the Dilaudid worked its way through my veins. It didn't occur to me to think about what I was going to do next. There was not much left in my bank account to find a place to stay to hold me over. Most of it went to Cookie and her stash.

"Where are you going now?" Cookie asked me while looking for a vein for herself.

"I don't know," I answered, feeling a little panicky all of a sudden. What was I going to do? I had no place to stay and no friends left.

344

The last place I wanted to end up was back in the apartment with Micah. In the spur of the moment, I'd summoned up all my bravery and walked away from him. Cookie's comment made me wonder if I should have given it more thought.

"You could stay here," Cookie suggested. "Pay half the rent and maybe drive me to doctor's appointments sometimes."

I said yes without hesitation and hugged the old woman. Not only would I be under the same roof as Cookie, I'd have full access to her Dilaudid. I could get high all morning, afternoon and night. If Cookie started getting stingy about her pills, I'd just steal them while she was sleeping and shoot up myself.

It seemed like the perfect arrangement. Sure, Cookie was a bit strange and frightening, but I believed I could handle it. Paying half her rent would be super cheap, and I'd have money left over every month for more pills. If Micah stayed in the building, we could keep our door locked and make sure he wasn't around before going outside.

While Cookie and I talked about being roommates, my cell phone rang repeatedly with Micah's calls. For the first time in as long as I could remember, I didn't answer a single one. He was probably sick as a dog, but that was his problem, not mine.

Hatred for Micah festered inside me, and it felt new and powerful. He deserved it after everything he put me through. I didn't stop to remember the mean things I'd done to him. If anyone was a victim, it was me, and I was sick of it. Micah was no longer necessary as part of my life.

He finally texted me instead of calling. "I feel really depressed," he wrote. "I'm afraid I might hurt myself."

The codependent part of me that was still attached to Micah felt afraid for him. I had a strong urge to go back upstairs and take care of him until he was okay. It was the way things always went, one of us crumbling and the other picking up the pieces until we broke all over again.

"I need to go to the psych hospital," Micah wrote in his next text. I tried to tell myself it wasn't my problem. Micah managed his life just fine without me before and didn't need his hand held. What if he really did hurt himself, though? Would I be able to live with that?

"I'll give you a ride," I texted back. "Don't think I'm coming back home or anything. It's just a ride."

Micah didn't say much in the car. He barely kept his eyes open and seemed severely depressed. I waited for him to yell at me for leaving him, but he never said a word. It looked like all the fight had gone out of him. I drove him to the same hospital I'd been admitted to after my suicide attempt.

"Good luck," I said as he opened the passenger door. I meant it more than I realized. Even though Micah made my life hell, I didn't wish him any harm. I hoped he'd find the peace he needed someday. We never found it together, but maybe second

chances were in store for both of us. I needed
to believe it.

Chapter Thirty-Four

When I got back to Cookie's apartment, she still hadn't returned home. It was getting late, and I had no idea where she was. I wanted to settle in for the night and maybe have her shoot me up before bedtime. I hadn't had any Dilaudid since that morning, and I was starting to feel the withdrawal from the short-acting drug.

It was important that I stay calm in front of Cookie. If I yelled at her about being late, she'd be less likely to give me what I wanted. I didn't want to rock the boat on the first night of being roommates.

I sat in a patio chair in front of the building and waited, almost falling asleep sitting up. A taxi finally pulled up about 1:00 a.m. Cookie rolled out of the back seat sloppy drunk. She paid the driver and came up the front steps where I sat under the outside light. Her breath smelled like alcohol. The stench of it made me nauseated.

"I just went up to the bar," she said, stumbling over her words. "Have you been waiting all this time? You poor thing."

"Yeah, but it's okay. I'm just glad you're back."

Cookie gave me a hug. Her body was sweaty from drinking too much, and I pulled myself away.

Cookie fumbled through her purse for her keys and came up empty. My withdrawal was becoming a throbbing ache. She spilled the contents of her purse onto the front steps, and I helped her look underneath the light. I silently cursed her for being so stupid.

"Oh, I probably left them at the bar," she finally said. "I'll have to get them tomorrow."

I tried to hide the irritation in my voice. "Cookie, I'm tired. How are we going to get in?"

"Maybe I left the back door open."

We walked around to the other side of the building and found the door locked. I was about to ask Cookie what our next move was when she hauled back and threw her purse through the door's four-paned window with a loud shattering sound.

I worried about one of our neighbors waking up to complain or even calling the cops. The noise sounded just like a break-in. Cookie casually reached through the shards of glass still hanging on the back door and unlocked it, as if it were the most natural thing in the world to smash your own window in the middle of the night.

My concerns faded as I followed her inside, knowing that I was closer to getting high. That mattered more than anything else. Cookie threw herself on her twin bed with a huge sigh. I was afraid she would pass out, and then I'd never get my drugs.

"Cookie," I called out. "Do you think you can help me for a minute?"

"Oh sure, honey. I just have to piss first."

I helped her to the bathroom. She left the door open, awkwardly pulling down her pants to sit on the toilet.

"Why don't you get the mix ready?" she suggested.

I'd never prepared a needle before, but I'd seen it done a million times. Surely, I could handle it. I reached into Cookie's purse where she kept the pills, taking out two from the bottle. Then I grabbed a spoon from the kitchen and a needle from the box in her bedroom.

My hands shook with anticipation as I crushed the pills into the spoon, adding a little water and then drawing up the mixture into the needle. Proud of myself, I brought the finished product to Cookie only to find her passed out on the toilet. An abhorrent smell filled the bathroom, making me gag instinctively.

"Cookie?" I said loudly, holding my nose. "Can you wake up?   I'm ready."

Cookie lifted her head as her eyes rolled

backward and she nodded yes. I knelt down beside the toilet and put my arm out for her. She took the needle from me, and her hand swayed as she tried to concentrate on finding a good vein. Was she even going to put it in the right way?

I pointed out a vein for her to hit, the awful smell still gagging me. Cookie managed to get the needle in my vein and pushed down the plunger. Sweet relief flooded me instantly, and I helped Cookie back to her bed where she passed out with her pants still half down.

As much as the pills helped me relax, I felt disgusted that I'd let Cookie shoot me up while she was using the bathroom. It was unsanitary at the very least. I felt I'd reached the lowest point possible, kneeling down in front of Cookie on the toilet like she was some sort of god I worshiped.

If it weren't for her drugs, I wouldn't have anything to do with her. Now I was actually roommates with this alcoholic junkie woman who had just put a purse-sized hole in her own window. What was the landlord going to say? Would he kick her out and me, too?

I stayed awake watching Cookie sleep as the drug wore off in my body. It made me feel sad to look at her. She was old and alone in the world. I'd never heard her speak about family or friends. She called me brave for leaving Micah, but there was nothing brave about where I ended up.

Even though I walked out on my husband, I still didn't have my children with me. My eyes flushed with tears as I thought about how much time had passed since Brandon, Shawn and Victoria were under my roof. I would never let them see me this way. Their mother was a disgusting drug addict, and they were probably ashamed of me. Someday I would end up like Cookie, alone in an apartment self-medicating to ease my pain.

I didn't remember the Glenna I used to be, the sweet, mild-mannered, naive young woman who seemed to have everything. There was no sense left of who I was or what I believed in. Although I claimed to love my children, what had I done to bring us

354

together? My life was controlled by drugs that demanded my attention above everything else and left no room for happiness. The honest truth was that I secretly wished I would overdose every time Cookie stuck a needle in my arm. Real life existed for other people, but not for me. I was caught up in a vicious cycle of using drugs to kill my pain and then the pain coming back tenfold.

I thought about the mistakes I made and the people I hurt. Living as a slave to my impulses, I automatically did the wrong thing before I even thought about it. Any money that ever came into my hands was wasted on impulse buys, illegal drugs and shopping sprees. I never thought about tomorrow, just instant gratification as quick as I could get it.

While it was true I was physically addicted to drugs, my mental addiction took its greatest toll on me. I thought of the times I half-heartedly tried to stop my substance abuse only to start again at the first opportunity. It was like the word "no" was not in my vocabulary, at least in any way that ever stuck.

My three children lived without me, something I never intended to happen. Any clarity I once had was clouded by the pain I felt inside, and so I decided to feel nothing. My heart broke into a thousand pieces anytime I ever thought about Brandon, Shawn and Victoria, but admitting they were better off without me was likely my bravest moment. They weren't safe with me the way I was.

They were literally the only reasons I wasn't dead already, not wanting to cause them even more pain. Suffering from mental illness doesn't happen in a vacuum. It sucks in everyone around you, and that was the last thing I wanted for my children.

Was it too late to change? Had I used up my last chance? I didn't plan to go back to Micah, but I didn't plan it any other time and always ended up back in our toxic relationship. I hadn't loved him for a long time, but he was also an addiction. Micah was right when he said he knew me better than I knew myself. I didn't know myself at all anymore. He knew exactly which buttons to push to get me to do what he wanted. Standing firm against him would be the hardest part. If I could do that, nothing else I faced would be as difficult. Nobody else could do it for me this time. The strength had to come from me.

As soon as the sun came up, I gathered my bags of clothes and makeup. Cookie was still passed out, and I tried to move quietly so she wouldn't awaken. Her kitchen floor was still covered in glass, but I didn't stop to pick it up. It wasn't my problem now. I stepped gingerly around it as I slipped out the back door and into my new life.

Chapter Thirty-Five

I drove away from Cookie's place with
nowhere to go but with a new resolve. I
spent the day driving around the
neighborhood trying to clear my head.
Suddenly, I felt a great urgency to start
climbing out of the hole I'd dug for myself.
Micah was still in the hospital, but even
when he came home I knew I wouldn't be
going back to him.

I tried not to think about all the bridges I'd
burned over the years. There was nobody
who would risk taking me in anymore, but I
definitely couldn't go back to Cookie's. I
finally pulled into the back corner of a Publix
parking lot and idled my car. The Florida
sun was hot and merciless, and I needed to
keep the air conditioner running. I scrolled
through my phone looking for a name to pop
up who might help with my current
predicament and came up empty.

Where would I sleep? How would I eat? A
million questions raced through my mind. I

couldn't just sit in the Publix parking lot forever. The police might show up and start asking questions. They wouldn't let me remain on the premises all night; that was for sure. I needed to find a real place to stay.

After a while, I decided to drive over to Club Oasis. The people at AA were kind to me before. Maybe they would have some idea of what I should do next. I asked the girl behind the snack counter if I could charge my phone. She agreed, and I plugged it in and stepped out onto the patio. How many times had I sat out there with Peter and Carol chatting about life, redemption and recovery? Everyone at AA was so friendly while I was part of the program, and I always regretted not keeping up with those friendships.

A pretty girl I remembered named Tatiana sat across from me with a group of young girls. They all had AA books, and I guessed Tatiana was doing sponsor work. I waited until the other girls left and sat down next to her. She was aware of part of my story already from the times I'd shared at meetings. I gave her an update about leaving

Micah and getting involved with Cookie. Tatiana was concerned that I was still addicted to drugs. Even though I cut off my own supplier, the urge to get high still nagged at me.

"You should call Robin and Paula," Tatiana said, pointing a finger at me.

I'd heard the women's names mentioned before. They ran a female sober halfway house in our city that had a reputation for being tough on the girls. I'd heard more than one girl crying on that very Oasis patio and complaining about Robin's strict rules and the punishments for breaking them. The thought of staying with those two ladies scared me to death, but it was better than being homeless.

"Do you really think I should?" I asked Tatiana meekly, afraid of what I was getting myself into. "It would only be for a few days, less than a week. When I get paid, I'll have enough money to get my own apartment."

Tatiana nodded and wrote down Paula's number. I was supposed to tell Paula that I was clean and sober but had no place to go and no money. I'd promise to pay her back for my stay when my paycheck dropped in a few days. Tatiana also told me to be honest with them about my addiction.

"Do you really want to stop using?" she asked me.

"I do," I answered, surprising myself. It was still hard to imagine getting completely clean, but I was willing to try.

Grabbing my phone, I went out to my car to make the call, taking several deep breaths before I dialed.

"Hi, I'd like to speak to Robin or Paula."

"This is Paula."

My voice stuttered as I repeated the words Tatiana told me to say.

Paula said I could come to their house immediately. I don't know why she believed in me and my story that day. I hadn't been the most reliable person in the world, but

this was a good time to start. Talking to
Paula made me feel less nervous about my
situation. Somebody had faith that I would
keep my word. It was more than I could
have ever hoped for. I asked Paula for
directions and arrived at their house ten
minutes later. Although I was still afraid of
her and Robin, I was almost too exhausted to
care. Withdrawal was settling into my bones
and making them throb with discomfort.

Robin greeted me at the front door with a
smile, telling me they already had a bed
waiting at one of their other halfway houses
nearby. She explained they ran six houses in
all with at least five girls living in each one.
When Paula supplied me with a one-page
list of the house rules, I impulsively reached
over and hugged her, making her jump in
surprise. Words failed me in that moment. I
had a bed to sleep in. I had never felt more
grateful.

The house I'd be staying in was only a few
blocks away from the main house, nestled
behind a row of trees so thick in the darkness
of the sky that I almost missed it. When I
knocked on the front door, a girl named

Jillian whom I'd seen at meetings opened the door and smiled at me.

"Hi there," she chirped. "Robin told me you were coming. I'll show you your room."

In the hallway, we passed several young girls furiously cleaning the bedrooms and bathrooms. It seemed strange as the hour was so late, but I smiled anyway as Jillian introduced me. The girls looked like they were all in their early 20s, and at age 40 I stuck out like a sore thumb. I felt ashamed of being a drug addict so late in my life when people are supposed to know better. Everyone looked at me with curious faces, but they were kind and welcomed me before going back to their scrubbing.

When Jillian and I reached my new room, I realized that it also functioned as a hallway for another girl's room. She and the other housemates ran continuously back and forth in front of my bed, giggling and whispering "sorry" every time they passed me. I was too tired to care and fell asleep over the covers still dressed in my jeans.

The next morning, I faced my current situation. I'd be getting paid soon, about 800 dollars. Maybe I could use it to find a small place that rented by the week. I wouldn't be spending money on drugs anymore, so I didn't envision my paycheck being eaten up to get high.

Even though I was only on my second day of withdrawal and physically felt miserable, I actually believed I could handle it. Still, it seemed scary to stay with Robin and Paula for too long. What if I messed up and got high and Robin and Paula drug tested me during my stay? I would feel like I let them down after everything they'd done for me.

Robin suddenly appeared in my doorway with her arms folded in front of her.

"I wish they hadn't put you in this room," she said, looking around. "Do you want to stay in one of the other houses? The ladies are closer to your age, and it's much more quiet."

I nodded my head yes right away. No offense to the other girls, but it was hard to concentrate with them running back and forth across my room. Maybe in the new house I'd fit in better and wouldn't feel old enough to be everybody's mother.

"It's on Ilex Street," Robin told me, writing the address on a scrap of paper. "I think you're going to love it."

I thanked Robin and gathered my clothes and makeup once again, throwing them in the back of my car. Ilex Street was just four blocks away, and Robin let me follow her over in my car. The house was large and inviting with a nicely manicured lawn and lime trees gathered along the walkway.

Robin led me inside and showed me to my new bedroom. A tanned woman with short blonde hair who looked about my age was sitting on the bed next to mine. I'd seen her before at AA meetings at Oasis, but we'd never spoken. She always seemed to be leading one of the groups. I was glad to be sharing a room with somebody who seemed to have her act together.

"Hi, I'm Kim," she said, stretching out her

hand to shake mine.

   I shook her hand back and sat down on
my bed. The house was quiet and smelled
clean like pine and lemons. I already knew I
was going to like it.   Kim and I chatted a
while before she had to leave for work. Once
alone in the house, I realized I felt serene for
the first time in ages, and this time it wasn't
because of drugs. The calm was coming from
within me.

Chapter Thirty-Six

Micah left the hospital with a renewed purpose to get me to come back home. He texted, emailed and called relentlessly, but I ignored all lines of communication. I knew the best thing I could do for both of us was to stay away from him. The little strength I'd built up inside myself was getting me through so far, but I knew it would disappear if Micah were back in the picture.

He texted one day to tell me our landlord was evicting him within 72 hours. It didn't surprise me as we hadn't paid full rent in months, but Micah was nearly hysterical.

"I can't be left homeless," he wrote. "You have to come back! Please Glenna, I need your help. We can still save the apartment."

The texts kept coming one after the other, and I knew they weren't going to stop. Micah's greatest fear was being homeless and left on the street. Being desperate made him dangerous. I couldn't tell him about the

Ilex house because if he found out, he'd show up on my doorstep. God knows what would happen after that.

Several days went by, and Micah never stopped trying to reach me. I had to admit I was worried about him. Where would he go? Would his drug addiction get worse and kill him? I was supposed to be getting my life together, but it still included him no matter how I tried to deny it. We could never be together again, but I still cared about his well-being.

The next time he called me, I picked up.

"Oh my God, Glenna!" Micah's voice was heavy and urgent. "I really need your help."

"Micah, you can't keep calling me like this. I'm sorry, but I've been clean for nearly a week. I refuse to screw it up."

Micah interrupted, "We can get clean together. We'll go to meetings every day if you want."

I turned away from the phone with a loud

sigh. He thought he still had power over me.

"I can't, Micah."

Micah's voice turned threatening. "Or I could kill myself," he announced. "That's always an option."

I felt anxiety rise in my chest.   It was important to stay strong, but what if Micah really did kill himself? I didn't know if I could live with that. The only thing I knew for sure was that if I went back to him, I'd probably be the one who ended up dead. I felt like a newborn baby finding her way in the world again. All of a sudden, I cared about what could happen to me. If I returned to Micah, I didn't have a scrap of hope.

"I'm sorry," I finally told him. "I'm not coming tonight or any other night. You have to stop calling me. I have to hang up."

Micah started bawling his heart out. It was painful to hear, like a wounded animal hurt on the side of the road. He begged me in between sobs to change my mind.

"I know you don't hate me, Glenna. Please help me. We can get through this together."

I said no to him one last time and hung up the phone on him.

I waited for the ringing to start again, but there was only silence. The guilt felt overwhelming, but I also felt a speck of pride for the first time in years. I'd chosen my life over Micah's. Things between us were truly over this time, and it felt like the sweetest taste of freedom.

Once I didn't have to worry about Micah, I spent the next few days focusing on my recovery. The withdrawal was bad as always. I was flooded with anxiety I couldn't control, and I kept as low a profile as possible. Robin and Paula didn't want the women staying in bed all day, so I forced myself to get up and interact even though it was the last thing I wanted to do. I was embarrassed the other ladies might have heard me throwing up or wandering around at all hours of the night because pain made it hard to sleep.

When my paycheck came, I had mixed
emotions. It would be bittersweet to have to
leave the Ilex house. I loved the people in the
house, especially my roommate Kim who
was so kind to me. She took me under her
wing from the first day and was there to
listen whenever I needed it.

Kim's compassion was appreciated at such
an uncertain time in my life. She taught me
how to be a real friend again and to think of
others before myself. I confided in her how
bad the withdrawal was, and she kept my
secret close to her heart so the other ladies
wouldn't find out.

I headed over to Robin and Paula's house
with money in hand. Paula greeted me with
a stern expression at the door, but I'd come
to realize that was just the way she looked.
Paula was a no-nonsense woman with a
strict moral code. Although she was nice, she
didn't put up with any bullshit. I liked that
about her and wished it would rub off on
me.

Paula let me in her house to give me a
receipt. She invited me to sit down, and I

thanked her and took a seat on the couch.

"Anyway," I piped up out of the blue, breaking the silence. "I've been clean and sober ever since I got here. I never thought I'd be able to say that. The withdrawal isn't so bad anymore, and I actually feel a little proud of myself."

Paula stopped writing and turned to look at me. "That's really good," she said.

"Well," I continued. "If I've come this far in only six days, I have to wonder what sixty days would look like."

Paula grumbled something and turned back to the receipt she was writing, but not before I saw the corner of her mouth turn up into half a smile. Everything was going to be okay, maybe even better than before. I felt overwhelmed by gratitude to have lived long enough to see an actual future without drugs and alcohol pulling the strings. Maybe that future included my children and I living happily ever after. I felt closer to it every day.

Chapter Thirty-Seven

At the Ilex house, I woke up early every morning and made my bed first thing. If Robin or Paula happened to come over, I wanted to make sure the bedroom was perfect. Their rules were strict but fair, and I made sure to follow every single one to the letter.

I went to Club Oasis for an AA meeting every day and was home by the 9:00 p.m. curfew at night. Most of my day was spent transcribing at my desk from my new home. It was important that I put some money away for safekeeping, especially if I wanted to be part of my children's lives again.

My chores in the house rotated every week, and I made sure to clean everything to Robin and Paula's satisfaction. They could show up for a random drug test or an inspection at any time, and I didn't want to give them any reason to regret letting me stay.

Things became routine in my life again,

and I thrived on it. It was a new way to live after being unstructured for nearly a decade. A regular schedule was exactly what I needed, and slowly it developed into habits that stuck. It almost felt like learning to walk and talk all over again.

I'd spent so many years with severe anxiety, waiting for the other shoe to drop because it always did. Once I started to relax and breathe more easily, I realized life didn't have to be a constant battle. I could persevere in the bad times and enjoy the good times just like everybody else.

My main focus was still my children and being back in their lives. Brandon and Shawn were older and settled into a life with their dad as the primary parent. I didn't want to shake up their world all over again, but thinking of our lost years made me feel so sad.

When I called to let Bonnie know I was in a halfway house, she put Victoria on the phone. It was hard to hear her little girl's voice asking when she could come home. I didn't have an answer yet. Even with the gains I'd made in recovery, I still couldn't afford to physically or financially take care of her or meet her needs. I prayed for the strength to get myself together faster so I could have her back home with me.

The women at Ilex became my lifeline. We'd gather out on the back patio every morning before breakfast and read passages from AA devotionals, each one of us telling what it meant to them. Kim was my constant companion. We giggled over TV shows and cooked meals together. It was like having a best friend again.

One day I came home to find she had redecorated our room, filling it with wildflowers, matching forest-green bedspreads and fluffy pillows. It made the place feel like a real home. I'd forgotten how it felt to belong someplace and have a loving "family."

Robin and Paula allowed Brandon and Shawn to spend the night after a few months. The first time Eric dropped them off at Ilex, I was overcome with emotion. The boys looked so much older, but when we were together it was like no time had passed as they both ran into my arms for hugs. They always believed in me even when I couldn't. If they were resentful at my absence in their lives, they didn't show it and instead showered me with love and affection. It made me feel like the whole world was full of possibility.

I didn't hear from Micah for several months. There was a small part of me that still worried about him, and I wondered if he managed to land on his feet. When he finally called, he told me he was living in Jacksonville with his best friend from childhood. The friend had driven down and picked him up from our old apartment right before Micah got evicted.

Micah asked about Victoria and said he called his sister a few times to talk to our little girl. It made me feel ashamed that I hadn't called her more frequently. Hearing her pleading with me on the phone to come get her was excruciating. We couldn't get through a single conversation without both of us ending up in tears.

Over the nine months at the halfway house, I saved enough money to find a place of my own. As much as I loved Ilex, I knew I couldn't stay there forever. There were women in early recovery who needed my bed more than I did. I found a lady in the want ads named Mary Ann who was renting out one side of her house in Jupiter. I'd have my own bedroom and bathroom and full use of the common areas. She said I could use her kitchen to cook, which was great because I didn't have so much as a plate to my name.

I told Mary Ann of my plan to have my daughter live with me again one day. Mary Ann said she would be happy to have Victoria stay there and when she did, I knew I'd found the right place.

Saying goodbye to Robin, Paula, Kim and all the other ladies was much harder than I thought. I promised to stay in touch with everyone and bring Victoria over to meet them all when she came home. I'd never be able to repay the debt I owed those women, but I wanted to honor them by paying it forward. Maybe all the things I went through weren't for nothing if what I'd learned could one day help somebody else. Even though I was still wobbly on my feet, the AA program was all about being selfless and helping others. Maybe one day I could be in a position to do that.

Whenever I was asked to tell my addiction story in a meeting, I agreed even though public speaking terrified me. I'd spent most of my life in hiding, so to come out and talk in front of people seemed like more than I could handle. My AA friends told me it wouldn't help just me, but also the people who came to listen. To my surprise, nobody judged or condemned me when I finished speaking about my past. It made me realize that folks in AA have all been there in one form or another with stories of hitting rock bottom. I felt compassion for those still suffering and grateful for those who made it out.

Sometimes I ran into Peter and Carol at meetings, but our relationship was never the same. They still felt burned by the way I used them and then abruptly left the program. Part of me wanted to beg them to let me back into their lives, but I knew I couldn't control how they felt. I'd have to wait until they felt comfortable with me again, if they ever did. Trust had to be earned.

I moved in with Mary Ann and concentrated on transcribing so I'd have enough money when Victoria came home. The only time I spent any money was when the boys stayed overnight. I'd cook them dinner and we'd watch movies or play with their video games. My moments with Brandon and Shawn were bliss, and I couldn't wait until the day they were reunited with their sister.

Now that I was away from Micah and clean and sober, Eric let me see the boys anytime I wanted. He eventually got remarried to a wonderful woman named Christine, whom I fell in love with the second I met her. She was warm and loving to my boys, and I believed Eric was lucky to find such an amazing wife. My grateful heart went out to Christine for taking care of Brandon and Shawn and loving them during the times I couldn't be there.

I continued my AA meetings at Oasis five times a week for lessons and fellowship. People remarked on how different I looked and acted from when I had first come into the rooms. I had to admit I felt like a new person or maybe a better version of the old Glenna. There was no more feeling sorry for myself and hating my life.

I stopped blaming everyone else for my problems and spent hours working on my fourth step in AA, writing out my resentments and trying to make some sense of them. It was hard to face the mistakes I'd made, but I knew it was crucial that I try. I sincerely hoped one day I could make amends to the people I hurt and truly forgive those who hurt me.

For the first time in years, I had some semblance of hope. Life didn't have to be miserable all the time. I could control my impulses and think before I acted. I felt confident enough to make decisions without somebody else's approval. The more strength I gained, the more I was able to make my own plans for the future. If I survived all the things that happened when I was taking drugs, maybe that meant I didn't need to be taken care of anymore. Over time, each day became more good than bad, and I continued to challenge myself to do the "next right thing" with every decision I made.

The more I learned in recovery, the more I realized that I hadn't been just addicted to drugs but also to Micah. We had become so intertwined that we thought we couldn't exist without each other. People asked me why I stayed with him as long as I did, and the only answer I could give was that he was the devil I knew. The thought of being alone and trying to manage my life, especially with my mental illness, seemed too frightening to even contemplate.

Loneliness was my worst enemy, a feeling so uncomfortable I went to great lengths to avoid it. I waited for years for somebody to rescue me from my miserable existence and absolve me of my sins. It wasn't until I had to rescue myself that I realized I never needed somebody else all along. The power to change had always been within me. I just had to find it.

I discovered that taking care of myself, getting stable and staying off drugs were truly a matter of life and death. For the first time in as long as I could remember, I chose my life.

Epilogue

Victoria came home to me for good near the end of 2013. When Bonnie couldn't care for her anymore, Victoria spent a couple of years with my mother in Missouri before I was finally strong enough to be a real parent. I didn't want to disrupt her life anymore and made sure she came home to a safe and stable household. The day I picked her up, she threw her arms around me, and it was like no time had passed between us. We soon settled into a routine as mother and daughter that we both desperately needed.

Shortly before that time, I met the man who is my loving husband today. Matt has been a blessing in my life since the first day I saw him across a crowded room at a mutual friend's gathering. When I told him about my past, he didn't judge me or put me down. Instead, he treated me like a princess and an equal and loved me without any conditions.

It was important to Matt early on that

Victoria and I reunite as soon as possible. We moved in together and set up a little girl's bedroom for when she came home to us. Victoria loved Matt at first sight. He is her father in every sense of the word. He calmed my fears about being a good parent with love and understanding. He also accepted my boys and found ways to include them in everything. With Matt's help, I got the chance to be a real mother again to all my children, not just for 30 minutes in a park once a month.

Matt came into my life at the perfect time. I wasn't looking for somebody to rescue me anymore, but I still think of him as my hero. Once I became the person I truly wanted to be, Matt gave me the freedom to express myself and go after my dreams. He urged me to forgive myself when such a task seemed impossible, knowing it was essential for me to move on from my past.

For the first time in my life, I experienced true love with another person. Matt didn't want to control or manipulate me. He encouraged me to become the best version of myself. After not being able to even sit still to read a book in my addiction, I started to heal myself through writing. It was a passion of mine since I was a child, and I was grateful it wasn't lost to me forever. In December of 2014, Matt and I eloped to Key West and got married on the shores of the Atlantic Ocean, and since then I've loved him a little more every single day.

I got an unexpected call in the spring of 2015 from Micah's mother. Through tears, she told me that Micah had died while fooling around down by the train tracks in West Palm Beach. A train had barreled past and hit him, killing him instantly. The police had found empty beer cans at the scene, which could explain why he had been acting so irresponsibly.

Part of me wondered whether he had jumped in front of the train on purpose, but I didn't say that to his mother. I always thought he was too much of a narcissist to go through with ending his life, although he had threatened it many times during our years together. He could have been more depressed than I thought, but either way we would never have any answers.

When I first heard the news, my emotions were mixed. Ever since Victoria came to live with Matt and me, Micah called us relentlessly and harassed us with the pretense of wanting to talk to his daughter. When he did get her on the phone, he yelled at her for not staying in touch with him as if it were her responsibility. By the end, Victoria refused to take his calls. She was still just a little girl. I felt very strongly about keeping Victoria away from Micah's drama. She'd been through too much already.

When Micah died, I felt a lot of unexpressed anger that I didn't know what to do with. My head was much clearer after we were apart a while, and I finally understood how much of our marriage was one giant manipulation. For so long, I believed I was worthless and crazy. It was Micah's way of keeping me down and part of the reason I always returned to him.

Once I gained some self-confidence, I realized how sick our relationship had been and to what extreme degree we had been codependent. I saw him for the first time through the eyes of my friends and family who warned me to stay away from him. Our physical distance, once he'd gone to Jacksonville, allowed me to be objective for the first time from the outside. Hundreds of wounds from his hurtful words and actions began to heal.

When Matt and I told Victoria about Micah's death, she was as composed as a young girl can be. Micah was never really a father to her, which must have made it harder for Victoria to relate. My little miracle is twelve years old now. She never mentions Micah anymore. When she's older and has questions about him, I'll make sure I'm open to talk about anything she wants. That doesn't include slamming Micah's memory or being mean, which my daughter might take to heart herself. I'll tell her about my mistakes and what I learned from them. Victoria is a survivor, and I'll always make sure she knows she has that power.

Brandon is a man now at 21 years old. He just graduated from college and has a truly amazing girlfriend who loves him dearly. He worked hard to become an Eagle

Scout, which he accomplished before his high school graduation. Brandon would be the first person I'd call if I were ever caught in a crisis. He's a born leader.

I expected Brandon not to trust me at first to make positive changes to my life, but he accepted me gladly with no conditions. Over time, I proved I could stay stable and in one place. I showered Brandon with love every day as ferociously as I could and tried hard to earn back his respect.

On the day he left for college 500 miles away from Jupiter, I drove to Eric's house and met Brandon in the driveway. As I was hugging him goodbye, I started to cry for all the time we missed. I held him tight and told him how sorry I was for all I put him through. Brandon looked me squarely in the eyes and told me to forgive myself because he already had.

Over time, it's become clear that he really meant it. Now, even as an adult, when Brandon comes back to town, he makes time to spend the night at my house so I can spoil him the way I always wanted to do.

Shawn is almost 17 and has become an intelligent, thoughtful and funny young man. He still lives with Eric, but he visits about every other weekend to stay overnight with Matt, Victoria and me. He's become an amazing chef who makes us gourmet dinners every time he comes over.

Shawn is a joy to be around and makes silly jokes just like when he was a little boy. I even got to teach him how to drive when he turned sixteen. His heart is humongous, and I would gladly slay any dragon for him.

Spending time with both boys again makes the once empty hole in my heart a little smaller every day. Eric has been a wonderful father to them, tough but understanding, and I give him so much credit for the men they turned out to be. I'm sincerely grateful for the sacrifices Eric made and for never cutting me off completely, which he easily could have done. Eric stepped up when I couldn't, and I'll always respect him for that.

I've had extensive cognitive behavioral

therapy to help me focus on my mental health and recover from past trauma. Researching bipolar disorder, I learned that the highs and lows I experienced were a factor in my reckless and dangerous behavior. I also have a side effect from the bipolar called impulse control disorder, which added to my bad decision making.

The diagnosis doesn't excuse any of the awful decisions I made, but I realize now how important it is that I stay stable. Taking my medications every day helps me cope with anxiety and depression. I know to pause and think before my actions. Taking care of my body is also important, so I try to eat good food and get enough sleep every night. Not every day is perfect, but my sense of well being has improved dramatically.

I still make mistakes like everyone does, but now I take responsibility and attempt to fix them rather than play the victim. There is happiness in the smallest of things: watching Matt cook breakfast in the morning, a productive day at work or listening to Victoria singing her heart out in the bathroom with her hairbrush as a microphone. Every day has special moments like this, and now I've learned to appreciate them rather than always waiting for something to go wrong.

For a long time, I didn't think I deserved a normal life after everything I'd done. I'm working on that, and I remember to always be grateful for second chances.

Matt and I recently made a trip to North Carolina to stay with my best friend, Susan, and her family. When Susan and I had a moment alone, she hugged me tight and said she was glad I was "back." It made me realize how far away I'd gotten from my true self, living a life that didn't fit me for years. It was as if the real Glenna was comatose or frozen in time. Susan confided she didn't think she'd ever see the real me again.

It almost felt like a rebirth, a chance to start all over again. I got to decide what was important to me. I could make decisions on my own with nobody influencing me. I grabbed hold of my precious life and cherished it this time. I'd never take it for granted again.

It's been over a decade since the night Eric told me he wasn't happy in our marriage. If I'd been honest about it, I wasn't really happy then either. My values and beliefs were all centered around another person, and I had no sense of who I really was or who I could be. There was never room to be myself until I finally made room. I know the woman I am today and actually like her, faults and all.

There's nobody in the world I'd rather be.

Made in the USA
San Bernardino, CA
21 February 2020